GO TEEN WRITERS

Stephanie Morrill & Jill Williamson

GO TEEN WRITERS

How to turn your first draft into a published book

N
teen

Go Teen Writers: How to Turn Your First Draft into a Published Book
Copyright © 2013 by Stephanie Morrill and Jill Williamson.

Library of Congress Cataloging-in-Publication Data
An application to register this book for cataloging has been filed with the Library of Congress.

The authors are represented by MacGregor Literary Inc. of Hillsboro, OR.

Cover Designer: Kirk DouPonce
Interior Design: Jill Williamson
Editor: Roseanna White and Chris Kolmorgen

International Standard Book Number: 978-0-9887594-1-1

Printed in the United States of America

To the writers who hang out
with us at Go Teen Writers.
Thanks for your creativity,
questions, and support.

Table of Contents

Step 2: Learning the Ropes of the Publishing Industry

Step 3: Putting Yourself Out There

Step 4: Finding a Good Literary Agent

Step 5: Building a Career

Extras: Lists and Resources

Hey, Teen Writers!

If you were hoping for a book from two writers who have this writing thing figured out, who have evolved beyond doubts, writers block, and insecurity, we're sorry to disappoint.

While we've designed this book to be used after you've completed a first draft, it can also be used as a roadmap for making sure you have the elements of a strong story. We've both pursued writing and publishing for about ten years now. While we still have a lot to learn, we've discovered a lot along the way, much of which we share regularly at GoTeenWriters.com.

The questions we're asked the most are, "How do I get published?" and "What should I do next?"

These are big, complicated topics. Too big and complicated for mere blog posts, we decided. Hence the book.

Everyone's journey is different, which we want to recognize and respect. Yet as we've reflected on our own journeys, and examined the paths of the writers around us, we've landed on a handful of steps that you can take to turn yourself into a card-carrying novelist. (Just kidding, there are no cards issued. But there may or may not be a secret handshake . . .)

Here's what we did to get where we are now

1. We wrote a good book and made it great.

Without this, you'll get nowhere.

We regularly hear from writers who are itching to get published but haven't yet completed this step. There's nothing wrong with looking toward the future and being excited about seeing your book on a store shelf someday, but that won't happen without a well-edited book.

2. We studied the industry.

Publishing is an industry with its own etiquette. Investing the time to learn it can save you a lot of embarrassment.

3. We created a book proposal and put ourselves out there.

4. We found good literary agents.

5. We learned to network with other authors and make connections with editors.

There you have them—Stephanie and Jill's five easy steps to getting published!

Just kidding.

The steps look simple and straightforward enough when you list them in such a way, but we all know getting published is anything but. Step one can take years, the industry is ever-changing, and finding and signing with a literary agent sometimes takes longer than getting a book contract.

It's easy to lose heart and look for shortcuts. The two of us certainly have. We can't make the process easy for you, but our hope is this book will encourage you to respect your dream enough to have the patience and endurance to stick with writing, and you'll find it to be a tool you can turn to time and time again when you're thinking, "Okay . . . what next?"

Stephanie and Jill

Step 1
Make Your Good Book GREAT

Make Your Good Book GREAT
The Macro Edit—Taking Care of Big Issues

If you've written your first draft, it's possible you've already built in many of these macro edit elements—like a strong cast of characters or a perfect setting. We included them here because sometimes when you edit your book, macro changes are necessary. It would have been helpful to us as new writers if we'd known early on how to edit these pillars in our stories.

A note from Stephanie

Both Jill and I have found it's best to take care of the big issues first—the plot, the characters, the theme—before you focus too much on scene tension and sentence structure. My friend Sally refers to it in housing terms. You would make sure a house had a strong foundation before you started painting it.

Something else Jill and I have in common is our bare bones first drafts. We both write quick first drafts and save our editing for after we type "the end." Ideally, I give myself six weeks off from a story before I start edits. This not only provides me time to do laundry and say hello to my family, it gives me enough space from the story to see it more clearly when I come back.

The first thing I do is read through my book in one or two sittings. I keep a notebook next to me and jot down the big things I notice—the plot line I foreshadowed in chapter two but never carried

5

through. The line in chapter twelve that has a special kind of weight to it, that I want to consider expanding into a theme. After I do that, I have a good idea of what needs work. Before I fuss with dialogue or tweaking each sentence, I first tackle those big issues I noticed.

I've always found the rewriting process to be one of the most exciting components of producing a great book. I originally ended this spiel with one of my favorite quotes about rewriting, only to discover Jill began hers with the same one. So I'll just let her talk.

A note from Jill

One of my favorite quotes is from author Michael Crichton. "Books aren't written—they're rewritten. Including your own. It is one of the hardest things to accept, especially after the seventh rewrite hasn't quite done it."

That's so true.

But I can't rewrite a book that doesn't exist—at least in a very rough draft form. So I write my first drafts as quickly as possible. That way, I have something to go back and fix.

I'm a visual learner, so the first thing I do after finishing draft one is go back through the book and list the chapters and scenes in order. This allows me to see the entire book on one or two pages so I can get a good idea of any plot holes. Then I think about my characters. By this time I know which ones I need to work on more, and I might spend a few days asking questions to learn more about them.

Once I've done all that, I start at the beginning and read, tweaking things as I go. I add description—since there's often little in my first drafts—I edit for each point of view character's narrative voice and dialogue, I often stop to research when necessary to get my details right, and I look for places I can insert plot points and references to my theme.

When I'm done, I go again. But more on that in the micro edit section.

I tend to rewrite as many times as I can before it's time to turn in the manuscript. The more the better.

There are no rules in writing. There are only guidelines.
—Nancy Kress

Thicker Plots

The Story Problem
by Jill

I don't want you to think that what Stephanie and I share in this book are rules that must be followed. Every writer is different and every story is different. That's what makes novels so great.

But there are consistent problems we see in the work of beginning novelists. And this book is meant to ask some hard questions that will get you thinking about what problems might exist in your story.

My first question is: What is your story problem?

I've read books where I was in the third chapter before I had a clue what was happening. And I'm not talking about a great suspense novel here, I'm talking about rambling on and on without any sign of a story problem.

The reader needs to know this so that he knows why he should care and keep reading.

The great thing about identifying your story problem is that you can use it as a quick pitch for your story. Here are some examples of story problems that sound like pitches:

A girl must fight to the death on national television. Twenty-four enter, one survives. (*The Hunger Games*) **Problem?** Fight to the death. **Why should the reader care?** Wants the main character to win.

An orphan girl comes to her new home only to learn that her new family wanted a boy. (*Anne of Green Gables*) **Problem?** The family wanted a boy. **Why should the reader care?** Wants the orphan girl to find a good home.

A hobbit inherits an evil magic ring and the enemy is coming to take it back. (*The Lord of the Rings*) **Problem?** Bad guys are coming to take the ring and with it could destroy everything that is good. **Why should the reader care?** Wants good to prevail.

If you want to hook your reader into your story, the reader needs to know the story problem as soon as possible. Because if your main character doesn't have a problem to solve, you don't have a story.

Make it Yours:
1. Can you identify your story problem?
2. Why should the reader care?
3. When does the reader learn the problem?
4. Could it be introduced sooner?

Story Structure
by Jill

It's possible you worked out your story structure back when you were plotting your novel, but if you haven't already, now is a good time to make sure your story works structurally. A good story needs a plot, which is the events that make up your story in order to solve your story problem. Most Hollywood plots follow a three-act structure that divides a screenplay into three parts.

Act one is the setup of the plot.

Act two is the confrontation, the emotional story behind the plot.

And act three is the resolution, where the plot and emotional story come together.

This works very well in novels too. I've put together a diagram of the three-act structure. As I walk you through it, I'll bold each of the areas from my chart so that you can refer back to it. I'm going to use the book *The Hunger Games* for an example since it's widely read. Just a warning, there will be spoilers as I break down the full three-act structure of the book. So if you haven't read it, go read it first!

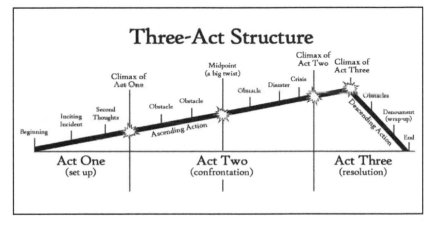

Act One: The Setup

Every story has a **Beginning** where the reader meets the main character, often in his everyday world before it changes. In *The Hunger Games*, we meet Katniss Everdeen on the day of the reaping. We meet her family and Gale, and we see her hunting. We get a glimpse of her normal life before it changes forever.

Next comes the **Inciting Incident**, which is sometimes called the opening disturbance. It's the event that happens, usually by the end of the first chapters, to get the story moving. In the reaping, Prim's name is drawn, and Katniss volunteers to take Prim's place.

And now we have a story.

The rest of Act One shows Katniss saying farewell to her family and preparing for the games and having some moments of **Second Thoughts**, which leads us to the **Climax of Act One**. This climax puts the main character at a crossroads. She must choose a course of action that will change the course of the story. She makes a plan and embarks upon it.

In *The Hunger Games*, Peeta declares his love for Katniss on national television. This is a major disaster for Katniss, who was already trying to fight her compassion for the boy who gave her bread when she was starving. How can she kill someone who loves her? And does he really? Or was it merely a plot to get the audience's sympathy?

This is a brilliant climax because it does so much in such a simple way. It raises the stakes for Katniss and Peeta, and it raises the expectations for the reader.

Act Two: Confrontation

Our heroine then sets out on her journey, meeting many obstacles along the way. In *The Hunger Games*, the games have begun. Katniss has gone off on her own to wait out the initial fighting and then the first major **Obstacle** comes her way: Peeta has teamed up with the Careers. Shortly thereafter, the fire to bring Katniss closer to the others is a major **Obstacle**, the result of which puts Katniss in the Careers' path (another obstacle). She climbs a tree and the Careers camp out underneath, waiting. Katniss is stuck.

Now we're at the **Midpoint** of the book. The midpoint is a bigger obstacle than the others and should end with some sort of **A Big Twist**. This midpoint scene in *The Hunger Games* with Katniss in the tree ends with two twists. First, Peeta saves Katniss' life when she'd thought he had sided with the Careers. Second, Katniss makes an alliance with Rue.

As we head into the second half of the book, the stakes are raised and we meet more obstacles along the way. Katniss and Rue make a plan to destroy the Careers' food supply. This is an obstacle they set for themselves. Then Katniss can't find Rue, which leads to the **Disaster**: Rue's death.

The disaster is what screenwriter Blake Snyder calls in his craft book *Save the Cat* the "All is lost" moment of the book, which pours right into the **Crisis,** also known as the "Dark Night of the Soul."

Snyder suggests that the "All is lost" moment should always include a whiff of death, be that the death of a character or a dream.

In *The Hunger Games*, Rue has become Katniss' ally. Her death is a disaster for Katniss, which leads to a crisis point. Where the disaster is action, the crisis is reflection.

The crisis is all about how your main character is feeling in regards to the previous disaster. It's the "Poor me!" moment and rightly so. It's that scene right before the main character reaches deep down and brings forth that last heroic push toward victory. This is the point when Katniss decorates Rue's body in her attempt to silently rebel against the games.

And now we have reached the **Climax of Act Two**. In *The Hunger Games*, the rule change is announced: Two tributes can win if they are from the same district. This pulls Katniss from her reflection on Rue's death, and she's energized. She must find Peeta. She must win the Hunger Games for Rue, for their districts, for Prim, for vengeance. She has a chance.

Act Three: Resolution

In the **Climax of Act Three**, the plot is at its highest escalation and slowly begins to unravel toward the conclusion. Our hero sets off to accomplish her new goal. More **Obstacles** stand in her way. Katniss goes looking for Peeta, finds him injured, and is determined to help him heal. And as the other tributes are killed, it's soon down to three: Katniss, Peeta, and Cato. And once Cato is gone and the Mutts destroyed, the new rule that two tributes can win is revoked. Will Katniss die or win the Hunger Games? She uses the berries to force the Capitol to choose for her.

The **Denouement** or wrap-up occurs after the climax. *Denouement* in the literal French means "the untying." This is the final outcome of the overall plot, where all the loose ends are tied up. Katniss and Peeta are heroes, but as they travel home, they see they've stirred up trouble. Katniss' trick with the berries has put her loved ones in danger from the Capitol's wrath, and now she must continue to fake her love for Peeta. A bittersweet **End** because it's the first book in the trilogy.

Every book's structure will vary some, but using the three-act structure will give your story a strong frame to build around. I've always found that planning a foundation doesn't squash my creativity; it forces me to tell a stronger story.

The Hunger Games Plot Chart

Beginning: Katniss and her family prepare for the reaping ceremony.

Inciting Incident: Prim's name is drawn. Katniss volunteers to take Prim's place.

Climax of Act 1: Peeta declares his love for Katniss on national television. How will she kill him now?

Obstacle: Peeta is working with the Careers.

Obstacle: A fire forces Katniss out into the open.

Midpoint Twist: Peeta saves Katniss' life, and Katniss forms an alliance with Rue.

Obstacle: Katniss and Rue set out to destroy the Careers' supplies.

Disaster: Rue is killed.

Crisis (Dark Night of the Soul): Katniss reflects on Rue's death.

Climax of Act 2: New rule: Two tributes can win if they are from the same district.

Climax of Act 3: Katniss offers the poisonous berries to Peeta. If they both can't win, no one will.

Denouement: Katniss and Peeta are heroes, but there was a price.

End: The Capitol is not pleased.

Make it Yours:

1. Using the example of *The Hunger Games* plot chart as a guide, create a plot chart for your manuscript with the blank one in the Extras section of this book. You can also download a larger one at:

www.jillwilliamson.com/teenage-authors/helps/

2. How does your chart look? Could your story use an obstacle or plot twist?

Writing the Cream of Your Story
by Stephanie

Many writers, including myself, find the middle of the book the hardest part to write. *Shouldn't the middle of the story be the best?* This thought plagued me as I worked on a story last year. It was a typical Stephanie story. The kind that's about a girl . . . and it's summertime . . . and she has this Big Problem . . . oh, and there's this guy . . .

Also in typical Stephanie fashion, I wrote the first couple chapters without a hiccup. But as my main character made her choice to go on her journey, the one that would lead her to the ending, I ran out of steam.

For the first time (and this was the eleventh novel I'd completed) I had a disturbing thought going on in my head—the middle is where all the story stuff happens. It should be the best part of writing. Why is it the part I dread?

Then one day, weeks later, it finally clicked for me—middles are hard *because* that's where all the story stuff happens! And coming up with all those ups and downs, those twists and turns, takes work!

Say my story idea is a modern girl whose parents discourage her from going to college. That tells me two things about the timeline— my start and my finish. I'll need to start with my character at home, still at the age where she would be making college decisions. Those will be my first couple chapters. I don't have to follow through on anything quite yet, just show my main character's world, do some foreshadowing, and get her ready for her journey. And then the ending will be her going to college. Or not going to college.

The beginning and the ending must exist, of course, and they have their own unique challenges, but the middle is where your characters will spend most their time and energy. Jill's three-act structure chart is excellent, but I also like to imagine my plot as an Oreo cookie. A Double Stuf, preferably.

The beginning and the end are those chocolate wafers, and if they're not perfect, you can tell the balance is off.

But what's an Oreo without cream, and what's a story without a middle? Not only is the cream delicious in its own right, it's what binds the chocolate wafers together. They all work together to make one amazing bite, same as your beginning, middle, and end must all work together to make a complete story.

The first element you need for a strong middle is a clear goal for your main character, typically related to the "story problem" Jill talked about at the beginning of the chapter. So if you haven't determined your character's goal yet, now's a good time to do so.

When your main character has a goal, it means he's invested in the journey and you have stuff you can take away. He wants to attend a fancy university? You can take away his financial resources, his straight As, his college counselor. He wants to stop Evil McVillain from taking over the world? You can trap him, take away his team, or strip away his defenses.

Another way you can ensure yourself a strong middle or act two is to give your character several people, places, activities, or objects to love. We usually think of that being a character-enriching exercise, but if your character has at least two things he cares about, it's easier to build conflict within him.

For example, when my son was about 15 months old, he had two great loves in the world—me and his pacifier. (I learned the first time I referred to pacifiers on the blog that they go by many names including binkies or dummies.)

So we were on a family vacation and the poor boy was exhausted. I was on one end of the hotel room, and he wanted to be

14

with me . . . but his pacifier was on the opposite side. Connor would start walking toward his pacifier, then remember I was the other way and start walking to me, then remember he wanted his pacifier, and turn to walk the other way. And the whole time he was bawling.

You want to create this kind of conflict in your plot, but you can only do that if you've given your main character multiple things to love and care about.

Of course the story can't be doom and gloom the whole time or you'll exhaust your reader. Yet too many good things happening to your character will drain away the conflict. So how do you balance it? You use "the pendulum," where you swing from good news to bad news to good news and back again.

The pendulum is done very well in *The Hunger Games*, particularly when Katniss is in the arena. Jill talked about the scene in the midpoint of the book, the big crisis, so let's take a look at it.

- •Katniss is found by the Careers and runs for her life—that's bad.
- •She climbs a tree and it turns out they can't—that's good.
- •They decide to wait her out at the bottom—that's bad.
- •In the morning, Katniss discovers a hive of "tracker-jackers" hanging on a nearby branch—that's bad.
- •She cuts it down and it explodes where the Careers are sleeping— that's good.
- •In the process, she gets stung too—that's bad.

See what I mean? When the balance is done well, it makes those rays of sunshine brighter and those rain clouds darker.

The middle of the book is also a great time to add or subtract a character. Does your character have someone she can depend on? Someone who's always on her side? Try taking him away. If it's not the type of book where you can just "off" characters, take him away in a different sense. Maybe that person is absorbed with a new romantic relationship and no longer has as much attention for your poor main character.

For adding a character, can someone new move to town? Or get assigned to work with your character on a project? Or maybe you're not adding a completely new character, but just moving a character on stage.

In *Pride and Prejudice* we have examples of both. We have Mr. Wickham coming into town (brand new character) but later we also have Georgiana Darcy, whom we've heard about throughout the book, but whom we don't see until much later.

And there are few things I love more in the middle of a novel than a Big Reveal, which has a variety of forms:

•A misunderstanding coming into the light. ("All this time I thought Adam was the bad guy, but it turned out he was actually trying to save the main character's life! Who knew?!")
•A secret past. ("Oh, wow, Jake has already been married once before?!")
•That secret the main character has been trying to keep finally exploding. ("What's gonna happen now that they all know the prime minister is her father?")

The middle of the book is probably always going to be trickiest for me to bring to life on the page. There's no formula for easy middles, but I've found these techniques to be helpful in revisions, and I hope you do too.

Make it Yours:

1. In the first section, Jill asked you to think through your story problem. Does your story problem tie in with your main character's goal?

Characters can have goals they know about-like in *Tangled* when Rapunzel longs to see the floating lanterns that mysteriously appear every year on her birthday. They also have goals they don't know about, like Rapunzel wanting to experience true love and acceptance. Have you given your character a goal he knows to chase and a goal he don't know he's chasing? How severe will the consequences be if he fails?

2. Are there multiple people or places your main character cares about? If he had to pick, which would

it be? How can you make it to where keeping one means losing the other? What are some ways he could wind up with both and what are some ways he could wind up with neither?

3. Examine several key scenes from your manuscript. How's the balance of good events and bad events? Are you hammering your main character with an excess of bad news or making his life too easy?

4. You know that dull section about 40,000 words in? (That's where mine always is, anyway.) Can you add someone? Can you take someone away? Brainstorm specific characters and write scenes with them just for fun. Keep what you like and toss what you don't. Or, better yet, save it in a different document in case you want to use it later, even for another project.

5. Time to dig into your characters' secrets. What kind of pasts do your other characters have? Is there a way their pasts can somehow ensnare your main character? (The show *Downton Abbey* is masterful at this!) What about your main character? Is he holding a secret, and when would be the worst possible time for it to come out?

Creating Plot Twists
by Stephanie

Hopefully while you were writing your first draft, you had one of those moments where an excellent plot twist appeared—*poof!*—as if by magic. I love that. And while I have that happen sometimes, more often I have to work for my plot twists in the second draft.

After I've done my read-through and found a few dull spots that need livening, I pull out a pen and paper. Brainstorming works better for me like that, somehow. I make a list of everything that *could* happen in this scene.

Let's say I'm reworking a scene where my main character, Madeline, is having an amiable discussion with her friend, Jack, about some troubles with their mutual friends. Here's the type of list I might make for how to punch up this scene:

- •They could completely disagree instead of agreeing like they do now.
- •They could discover their friends are listening to this conversation.
- •Jack could ask her out.
- •Madeline could tell him she thinks her parents are getting divorced. (Are her parents getting divorced . . . ?)
- •Madeline could tell Jack she thinks they're being followed. Maybe they ARE being followed . . . who could be following them? What would they be after?

And so on. Sometimes I get a little goofy and write down stuff like *Jack falls and gets amnesia and now thinks his name is Fred*, but that's okay. It's brainstorming. A little goofy is okay and might lead to some kind of surprise breakthrough. But if you get way out there—*they're attacked by purple frogs*—you're not really helping yourself.

You'll notice toward the end of the list, I finally came up with a potential twist that I wanted to follow a bit more. It's possible I'll try it out and it won't fit for some reason, but it also might work.

Another thing I like to do—sometimes in the first draft stage but more often in the second draft—is try to come up with some unique, previously unknown connections between my characters. (This is an exercise I first read in *Writing the Breakout Novel* by Donald Maass, but I've adapted it a bit for my own needs, and I encourage you to do the same!)

For this exercise, I pull out a pack of index cards. I pick five or so characters and write one name on each notecard, then stack them in a pile, writing-side down. Then I pick five or so big(ish) events in the book, like "Madeline's birthday party" or "the first day of school." I write one event on each notecard, then stack them in a separate pile. And then I'll pick out a few settings from the story—the vineyard, the dry creek bed—and write those down in the same fashion, then put them in their own pile.

Sometimes I spread the cards flat like I'm playing a game of Memory, and sometimes I keep them in piles and just draw the top card. Either way, you want to pick three cards. Maybe one from each category, or maybe it'll be more fun to pick from the same category. Your choice!

When combined, the cards typically make no sense. I might end up with Madeline's dad, the first day of school, and the vineyard. Those are three things that never intersect during the story, but then I sit there and try to come up with ways that I *could* make them intersect. And if not all three of them, maybe two. Is Madeline's dad at school for some reason on the first day? Why? Or is he at the vineyard? What could the first day of school and the vineyard have in common?

Once I've exhausted possibilities, I set the cards aside and draw a new set. I've found this is a great way to get me thinking creatively about my story, and I always walk away with something I love and never would've thought of otherwise.

This can also help you to fill in the "gaps" if you've spotted big holes in your story. Jill has another thought on how she does that.

Filling in the Gaps
by Jill

I get emails from teen writers who are frustrated with how to move forward with their stories. Some have finished books that are far too short to ever be a novel and want to know how to make their books longer. And some are stuck because they have ideas they love, scenes they've written, but there are big holes in the story that keep it from moving forward.

When this happens to me, I need to turn on my imagination and spend some time brainstorming. But before I do that, I write out a plotting chart like the one I created for *The Hunger Games*. But since this one isn't complete, I leave lots of spaces in between the plot points I already know. Then I sit down with a pencil and brainstorm what things might be able to happen in between the scenes I've got. I think about each character's motivation and what each might do that will get them from one scene to the next. I think about things the antagonist might do to get in the way of my hero accomplishing his goal.

Here is an example from my first book, *By Darkness Hid*. The typed text are the scenes I already had, the handwriting is what I filled in after brainstorming. Forgive the spoilers!

By Darkness Hid Plot Chart

Beginning: Achan gets into a fight while milking the goats. We meet Riga, Harnu, Poril, and Sir Gavin.

Inciting Incident: Sir Gavin offers to train Achan as his squire, even though it's against the law for slaves.

-Achan starts training as a squire, learning to use a waster.

-Achan discovers that Gren (the girl he loves) is to marry Riga.

-Sir Gavin suggests that the tonic Achan drinks is poison.

-Sir Gavin sends Achan to kill an animal and carry it back.

Climax of Act 1: Achan is declared a squire, but Prince Gidon is threatening to make Gren his mistress.

Obstacle: Poril demands that Achan help in the kitchens for Prince Gidon's coming-of-age celebration, but Sir Gavin tells Achan to compete in the sword fighting tournament

-Achan meets Lady Tara, Lady Jaira, and Bran Rennan in a game of Hoodman's blind.

-Lord Nathak discovers Achan is Sir Gavin's new squire and sends him back to Poril in the kitchens.

-Sir Gavin introduces Achan to Prince Oren.

Obstacle: Sir Gavin has vanished and Achan must now serve as Prince Gidon's sparring partner.

-When Achan sees Lady Tara in the stands, he chooses to beat Prince Gidon in a sparring match and is whipped for it.

-Prince Gidon asks Achan to bring Gren to him to serve as the prince's mistress.

-Achan confronts the goddess Cetheria in her temple, but hears Arman's voice instead.

Midpoint Twist: Achan saves Gren from the prince by urging her marriage to Riga to happen right away.

20

-Prince Gidon discovers Gren's recent wedding and threatens to kill her if Achan ever leaves his service.

Obstacle: Prince Gidon leaves for Mahanaim and demands that Achan come, leaving his home forever.

-A person with a scratchy voice speaks to Achan's mind. Achan doesn't want to believe in Bloodvoicing, but it seems clear that he has the gift.

-Silvo Hamartano and his friends beat up Achan.

-Bran befriends Achan and offers to let him join the Márad, a rebel group that is opposed to Prince Gidon. Achan refuses, fearing for Gren's safety.

-Achan sees the memorial tree, the place where King Axel was killed.

Disaster: Poroo attack Prince Gidon's procession and Achan is struck down.

Crisis (Dark Night of the Soul): Accused of trying to kill Prince Gidon, Achan sits in the dungeon knowing he will never be free.

-Achan befriends Vrell, a healer boy with the scratchy voice who had been talking to him on his journey.

Climax of Act 2: Achan is rescued from the dungeon by Kingsguard knights.

-Vrell is held hostage for Achan's return, so he and the knights stage a rescue.

Climax of Act 3: Sir Gavin takes Achan before the Council of Seven and makes a shocking claim.

-Prince Gidon tries to kill Achan. Bran and Sir Rigil rescue him.

Denouement: Achan and the knights fight Prince Gidon's soldiers to get out of the castle.

End: Achan and the knights flee into Darkness to avoid Prince Gidon's wrath.

While figuring out what happens in your stories can be exciting, it can also be frustrating when a twist isn't working like you hoped it would, or when a scene is flat but you don't know how to make it better. Brainstorming with a friend, or exercises like the ones above, can help a lot. Sometimes the results are instantaneous. But if they aren't, don't be discouraged. Often the right solutions to story problems take time and energy and digging.

Make it Yours:

Go back to your own plot chart and see if you can brainstorm some new scenes to fit in between the scenes you already have.

A character is no more a human being than the Venus de Milo is a real woman. A character is a work of art, a metaphor for human nature.
–Robert McKee

2 Deeper Characters

Main Characters:
Someone Worth Following
by Stephanie

Something we commonly get asked is, "Can you have more than one main character?"

While there are books that have more of an ensemble cast, we would advise one main character. Especially if this is early in your writing journey. Readers need a character to latch onto and cheer for. With an ensemble cast, it can be tough for readers to bond because they aren't getting as much page time with each character.

I once had a meeting with a teen writer where she told me she had seven main characters, but later I figured out she meant that she actually had seven *POV* characters. So let's clarify right off the bat that the reader can view the story from a variety of angles, a variety of points of view, but still there would be one main character. This is commonly done in the romance genre, where the hero and the heroine share the stage almost equally, but typically the heroine is still the main character, still the driving force of the story.

How do you know who the main character should be?

The answer is whoever has the biggest change to go through. Who has the most at stake in the story? Certainly you will have other characters that play huge roles, who are going through changes themselves, but which character's goal is driving the story forward?

This brings us back to the importance of giving your character a goal. The first time I heard that concept, it was a light bulb kind of moment.

A goal! Then my character will have something to *do*! Brilliant!

The goal should not only propel your character through the book, it should draw the reader into the journey. If you've done your job right, readers care about the character's goal and want to see him achieve it. They cheer when things are going well, and they weep when things are going poorly. Consider the Lord of the Rings trilogy and Frodo's goal of returning the ring to the fires of Mordor. It has everything a character goal should have:

- •High stakes—Bad stuff will happen if he doesn't do it.
- •It's noble—It's something he *should* want to do.
- •Others come alongside him—Your character will need cheerleaders.
- •There's opposition—It should be a strong enough goal that others *don't* want your character to reach it.
- •It's achievable . . . but he can't do it alone—If the goal is too easy, the reader will lose interest.

Make it Yours:

1. Consider your main character's goal. Do the five things listed above apply to it? If not, how can you make them happen? Take a few minutes to brainstorm.

2. Asking "Why?" is the best tool you have for deepening characters. *Why* must he achieve this goal? *Why* does it matter to him? *Why* is he willing to risk everything to achieve this? When working on your character's goal, use "why?" to dig deeper.

Your main character not only needs a goal, she need an inner desire.

For this I'm talking about your touchy-feely words. Love, respect, contentment, peace, acceptance. In her soul, your main character requires something, thirsts for something. Maybe she knows it. Maybe she knows she's materialistic, and she's searching for contentment. Or maybe she doesn't know. Maybe she doesn't realize how deeply it scarred her that her mom was a workaholic. That's for you to decide.

Often the inner desire is tied directly to the character's goal. Like a character whose goal is to find her birth mother would likely have a corresponding inner desire for acceptance. But sometimes the inner desire and the outer goal can be seemingly at conflict with each other. What about a warrior whose goal is to win the battle, but whose inner desire is for peace?

What lie does he believe?

One of my favorite aspects of developing or enriching a character is to give him a lie to believe and a reason to believe it. In Melanie Dickerson's *The Merchant's Daughter*, the hero believes beautiful women cannot be trusted because he was spurned once by a beautiful woman. The heroine of that story is beautiful, though it's never brought her anything but trouble, and her conversations with the hero are often full of a bitterness she doesn't understand.

And just like the lie can be a point of weakness for your main character, it can be the downfall of your antagonists. Consider the Harry Potter books where the villain, Voldemort, has basically bought into his own press. While he believes several lies, the one that hurts him the most is he thinks he's so clever that he's the only one who can find certain places or do certain things. The result is he underestimates Harry and his abilities.

Make it Yours:

1. What does your character fear, and how can you make it come true?

2. What lies does she believe?

3. What's a secret desire your character has that she has never told anyone?

Writing a Strong Antagonist
by Jill

As we've touched upon, the most important thing you need to decide about any character in your book is: What does he want desperately? And how am I going to keep it from him?

This shouldn't change when dealing with your antagonist. The antagonist is the villain, by the way, but he needn't be evil incarnate. He might be a nice guy. If two best friends were going to try out for the track team, but there was only one position available, they'd instantly become each other's antagonists. An antagonist is merely the character who stands in the way of your hero achieving his goal.

Your antagonist can be likeable. The best villains are those the reader can relate to in some small way. Yes, he's trying to stop the hero, but if the reader can understand his twisted logic, he'll be even more powerful.

Make it Yours:

1. Take those questions you answered for your main character and answer them for your antagonist. Your antagonist needs ambition and goals too. He should be plotting and planning, not just taunting your main character. He thinks he *is* the main character!

2. If you were telling the story from the antagonist's point of view, what would the beginning, middle, and end be for him?

The Rest of the Cast
by Stephanie

One of the things I struggled most with as a new author was developing a robust cast of characters. I had given oodles of thought to my main character, somewhat less thought to my antagonist, and then my other primary characters were really there just to populate the story.

I think this mistake is common because we don't want anyone to outshine our main character. That's who we're all here to see, right? Everyone else is only there to support the main character and guide him (or oppose him) on his journey.

While the focus should be your main character, and all storylines should somehow relate to him, keep in mind that *everybody* thinks they are the main character. Your main character's best friend doesn't think of herself as "the best friend." She thinks of herself as the main character, and that the main character is *her* best friend. Make sense? This means that the best friend has life goals same as the main character does. Not only does she have goals, but so do the other friends they hang out with. And the main character's parents. And the main character's wicked boss. The other characters in your novel should have goals they are taking steps toward achieving.

Now, maybe not *everybody* in your novel needs a goal. The receptionist at the office who says two things during the entire book might not need something to work toward, but consider giving her a problem. It could be that her car wouldn't start this morning, or that she dropped her cell phone in the toilet. Just something that keeps the dialogue from being boring ("Hi, how can I help you?") and from being all about the main character.

Everybody brings their own unique baggage into a conversation. That means everyone hears things differently. I'll never forget having dinner with a friend and her new boyfriend, who I was meeting for the first time. He was sharing a story about work, and my friend interrupted him with, "You didn't tell me you went there. You totally lied to me!"

Do I even *need* to tell you my friend had once been badly burned by a cheating boyfriend? She heard her new boyfriend's words through the filter of her past, like we all do. And it affected the conversation.

When your characters are in conversations, think about where they've been and where they hope to go. Characters who grew up in stable, loving families will react to conflict differently than characters who grew up in abusive households. Someone who's been scarred in relationships might be suspicious and untrusting. Someone who desires money and power might be charming if you have something he wants, but cold and dismissive if you don't.

This filter is also what makes characters talk differently. Making characters sound unique is tough. After all, they're all passing through the filter of *your* head. This is something that's easier to obsess over during the micro edit, after I've spent a lot of time with these people. We'll address it more then. For now you're just making sure their backstories are in place.

Make it Yours:

Sometimes our characters all sound the same because we haven't taken the time to get to know them. Lots of authors use interview sheets, but those have never worked well for me. Partly because I find it boring to write out every character's favorite color.

In *The Art of War for Writers* by James Scott Bell, he talks about writing character journals. I completely fell in love with this exercise because it doesn't feel like meaningless paperwork, it feels like writing, like creating.

You can do them for your main character, of course, but it's *really* fun with secondary characters and the antagonist. Ask them "How do you feel about your name?" "What's your relationship with your mom like?" and then they just take over. Usually for pages. Because you're writing in first person, this works wonders for solidifying their voice and motives.

Still round the corner there may wait, a new road or a secret gate.
–J. R. R. Tolkien

3 Richer Settings

Picking the Right Contemporary Setting
by Stephanie

If you can pick up your story, move it somewhere else, and it wouldn't change a thing, you haven't found the right setting yet.

But how do you know what the right setting is for a book set in modern times?

Sometimes it's simply a gut thing. Maybe you have something you want to say about your hometown, so you set it there. That's fine. Stephen King, you'll notice, has a decent amount of books set in Maine.

But if you're struggling to find the right locale, here are some questions you can ruminate over:

What would be more uncomfortable for my main character?

That sounds like a cruel question, doesn't it? But if your character is comfortable in her setting, your story is in danger of becoming bo-ring. So how do you make her uncomfortable?

29

If your character has an embarrassing family, consider sticking him or her in a small town, where everybody knows everybody's business.

If your character is desperate to stand out, to be noticed, try putting her in a big city or at least a big school where there's lots of competition.

If your character is poor, figure out a way to put her in a ritzy setting. Or the reverse can work great too: a character with tons of money who finds herself in a place where money can't do anything for her.

Should I make up a place?

Possibly.

This works particularly well for small town contemporaries, like in Betsy St. Amant's *Addison Blakely: Confessions of a PK* where we get the small town Kansas feel with the fictitious town of "Crooked Hollow" but you don't have the real life residents complaining that Got Beans is actually on the west end of town, and how dare the author suggest otherwise . . .

With this, however, you still have to be mindful of the regional culture. Going back to the Kansas example, you wouldn't want to say anything about buying wine at the grocery store (because they don't sell it in the grocery stores) or reading the license plate on the front end of the car (because they only have license plates on the back of their cars). Messing up those kinds of details will snap all your lovely, wonderful Kansas readers right out of your storyworld.

Consider the Intangibles

There are tangible things about where we live—the flora and fauna, the seasons, the cost of a gallon of milk—and then there are the intangibles. Living in San Francisco, California is completely different than living in Dallas, Texas. Both are big cities, but the politics and the cultural priorities are different. When meeting someone for the first time, you would make different assumptions about them if you learned they were raised in Dallas than if they were raised in San Francisco.

Wherever you choose to set your story, you must identify your character's emotions about where he lives. We all have a relationship with where we live; we have feelings about it. And sometimes our feelings conflict with each other—one day we might love that we know so many people in our town, that we can hardly go to the grocery store without bumping into someone we know. Another day, we might loathe that same thing.

If you build that into your characters, not only will your reader connect with your unique setting, you'll breathe life and movement into your story.

Make it Yours:

1. Consider your current story setting-what's the opposite? How would your story change if you moved it there? Take a few minutes to brainstorm. Try writing a scene where your main character is in this opposite setting. How does it feel? Did you learn anything interesting about your character or your original setting?

2. Make a list of three things your character likes about where he lives and three things he doesn't like. First consider the things he likes-what are situations in which he'd cease to like those? Now consider the things he doesn't like and do the same. How could he come to like those? (An excellent example of this is in *Twilight*. Bella originally loathes the constant rain of Forks, Washington, but because the rainy days are the ones when Edward comes to school, she comes to look forward to them.)

Creating a Mythical Storyworld
by Jill

Stephanie's advice of making the setting uncomfortable for your character applies to mythical storyworlds too. Your reader experiences your storyworld through the characters, so any way you can connect character and environment will strengthen your story.

When creating a mythical storyworld, your imagination is the limit. That might seem a little overwhelming at first, so here are some ideas to get you started.

1. Pick a time period to model. Medieval, space in the future, ancient, renaissance, regency, the old west, contemporary, future on earth.

2. Pick a genre. Fantasy, science fiction, dystopian, time travel, steampunk, supernatural, paranormal, apocalyptic, etc.

3. Will this time period and genre create the right storyworld for your plot to work?

4. Consider the rotation of the planet. How long is a day? How long is a year?

5. Is there a country in the world or throughout history that you could use as a model for the style of government you'd like to portray in your story?

6. Is there a country you could use as a model for the terrain, climate, vegetation, and wildlife in your story? You don't have to use everything, but keep in mind what will be realistic and logical to readers. Having a moose show up in a desert might jar the reader out of your story. An oddity here and there *can* work, but if you have too many inconsistencies, you risk losing the realism of your world.

7. Are humans the only type of people in your story, or will you have other beings who speak?

Using Maps and Floor Plans

You may not be an artist, and that's okay. But sketching out a map of your storyworld can be really helpful. I've also found it useful to grab some graph paper and sketch out floor plans for character's homes or facilities or castles used in my stories. Here's a link to maps and floor plans I've made: www.jillwilliamson.com/maps

As you can see, my maps are not all nice and tidy. Some were just to help me visualize the layout so I could describe things.

> ### Maps Can Help You Plot
>
> When you spend time drawing a map and adding in details, you'll come up with plot ideas. Where you place things on a map can have an effect on your plot.
>
> For example, if there are two cities close to the only road that leads out of a mountain pass, that might create discord between the two cities as they fight for access to the road.

When I started to brainstorm my Blood of Kings trilogy, all I knew about the land was that half of it was covered in constant darkness and there was a half living/half dead tree in the middle of the land. But I wanted a map. So I took a blank sheet of typing paper and drew a craggy shape. It was a little too big and looked a lot like Africa, so I erased a bit to get a more unique outline. Then I added a bunch of dots to indicate cities. I added about forty dots.

That seemed like way too many cities to have to name. So I erased half of them.

Better.

I shaded my half-darkness over the land. I added roads, rivers, and mountains. I added my half living/half dead tree.

I still needed to name all the dots. But how do you come up with name for the cities in your storyworld?

There are lots of ways. Tolkien invented his own language. Some people use street names. Some use a phone book to find interesting names. You could use a map of earth, pick a foreign country, and choose names of cities, rivers, or mountains. (You might want to look up the meaning of foreign words just in case you chose one that has a troublesome translation.)

J.K. Rowling used Latin for many of her character names and for most of her magic spells in the Harry Potter books. I thought that was clever, so when I was working on my map for *By Darkness Hid*, I looked on my bookshelf and saw a French dictionary and a Hebrew/Greek concordance. I thought Hebrew/Greek sounded more fantasy-like than French—it sounded kind of Klingon. Plus, I liked the idea of using words from the Bible.

So I went with it. For example, "allown" is Hebrew for "oak" or "tree." Guess what I named the city where my half living/half dead tree is? Allowntown. And "er'rets" is Hebrew for "earth," the same word used in the Bible here: "In the Beginning, God created the heavens and the *earth*." So I named my fantasy world Er'Rets.

I like having hidden meanings.

But I didn't want to name everything Hebrew because it's really hard to pronounce. So I came up with some more tricks. I gave each town a theme for brainstorming names. Allowntown, for example, is an orchard town. I wrote a list of types of apples: Gala, Pippin, Cortland, Concord, Crab, Ginger, Fuji, etc. And when I needed a new character from Allowntown, I picked a name from the list.

Carmine is a vineyard town, so I made a list of things having to do with wine: Rioja, Flint, Terra, Keuper, Pinot, Concord, Malbec, etc. For Berland I used Inupiat names. For Magos I used Gaelic names. For Cherem, I used names of stars. For Nesos, I used Hawaiian names.

I also created a chart for each city. I used a set of encyclopedias to look up similar places. For example, the landscape and climate of Barth is similar to northern Africa. So I looked up some countries in northern Africa and jotted down climate, crops, animals, plants, industry, that sort of thing. That helped me understand what it might be like to live in Barth.

I did this for every town in my land. If you'd like to see the chart I used, download the Storyworld-Building City Chart from my website: www.jillwilliamson.com/teenage-authors/helps.

Make it Yours:

1. Draw a map for your storyworld. Add cities and other landmarks. Name them.

2. What have you done to make your world unique?

3. Did drawing the map help you think of new plot ideas? If so how?

Write a History

If your world is going to feel real, it needs more than a map and cool names. Write out a history of your land. Go back as far as you want. For inspiration, Google the history of our world. Look at the different eras and see how we've advanced over the years.

I wrote a history for Er'Rets starting 500 years before my story began, when the first king came to the land via a ship. I created a timeline of who was king when and what major events took place: wars, births, deaths, etc. I also wrote family trees for the lords of each major city so that I knew who married who.

All this gave my land character. For example, I knew why the people from Cherem hated the people from Magos. They'd been battling for years. And if a Cheremite and a Magosian were to meet in my book, it might get ugly.

And ugly is good because ugly means conflict.

Create Rules and Magic for Your World

Laws of nature make things possible or impossible on our planet. The same should be true of your world. Think about the environment, any different types of beings you've invented, and magic. For each of these things, there must be rules. Without rules, you lose realism.

In my book, I created a magic called bloodvoicing. It's a telepathic magic that runs in one's blood, genetically, like blond hair or blue eyes. Bloodvoicers can speak to other bloodvoicer's minds, but they can also listen in on non-gifted individuals. Bloodvoicers can learn to fight with their gift as well, forcing a person's soul from their body.

It was this ability that forced me to create different laws of nature for my storyworld. I invented the Veil, a spiritual realm bloodvoicers could travel through if they left their bodies. The Veil was the place between life and the afterlife, and so when someone was in the Veil, his soul was pulled in one of two directions.

There are other rules I created for bloodvoicing, but I hope you get the idea.

If you do add magic to your story, consider the source of the power and how the characters are able to harness it. Rumpelstiltskin, from the ABC show *Once Upon a Time,* often says, "Magic always comes with a price." If you create a price for magical ability, you'll increase the conflict and risk for your characters, which makes the magic more believable.

Maybe you don't have magic in your story, but perhaps a race of people has the ability to walk through fire. Maybe your planet rotates faster than earth and the days are shorter. Could be that the climate of your planet is hot and all natural water is near boiling. Maybe your spaceships don't require warp speed because they can teleport from one location to another.

Your imagination is the limit.

A Note on Language

Many editors are wary of fantasy novels that are thick with languages the author invented. Most readers want a character-driven story. You can have many different languages spoken in your storyworld, but you don't have to actually invent these languages á la Tolkien or Marc Okrand (Klingon). Spend the majority of your time learning to write and rewrite a great novel. Then, if you really want to invent a new language, go for it. Just make sure that it enhances the story and doesn't take over.

Don't get stuck on creating the storyworld

Taking the time to brainstorm your storyworld does two important things: it makes it easier for you to write about your storyworld, and it makes your storyworld feel more authentic to your reader. Consider making a three-ring binder with dividers for different cities, languages, history, or creatures to keep everything organized and easy to refer back to.

You could spend months or years brainstorming a fantasy world. Have fun, but make sure you don't get stuck here forever and forget to write the book!

Writing Historical Fiction
by Stephanie

I once tried writing a historical. I wrote about 500 words of the first chapter and had about 500 questions written down. I learned that while I adore reading historical fiction, I probably don't have what it takes to write it.

Historical fiction is a wonderful blend of history and story, and—like with fantasy and sci-fi—you have the privilege of transporting the reader to a completely different time and place. It's a privilege you should take seriously, which is why it's so important to be accurate in your facts. Yes, it's fiction, but readers are smart, and if you're fudging details or flat-out making up stuff, you'll rip them out of the storyworld and probably lose a reader forever.

As important as it is to be accurate with your details, you also have to keep in mind that a reader picks up a novel for a good story, not a history lesson. During your research, you'll discover tons of fascinating details and you'll need to watch yourself for info dumping. It's a very difficult balance.

Another tricky thing is appealing to the modern reader while being true to the mindset of that time. While it's commonplace for us to see women working outside of the home, to see girls getting the same education as boys, it's likely unheard of in the period you're writing. Keep in mind that your characters won't be shocked by it, but you'll need to present the issues in a way that a modern reader can still relate.

A great way to get a feel for a different period of time is to read literature from then. If you're writing regency novels, pick up a few books by Jane Austen or the Brontë sisters. This will really help you tune in to the time you're hoping to accurately portray.

And www.etymonline.com is your new best friend because it will help you research the root of words and when they came into use. That way you'll know if it's okay for your character to say, "Wow!" in your Colonial American novel. (Which it is, because surprisingly "Wow" dates back to 1510!)

People ask me when I start one of these projects, what is your theme? I haven't the faintest idea. That's why you're writing the book, it seems to me, to find out.
—David McCullough

4 Weaving in Your Theme

Digging Out Your Themes
by Jill

When I attend writers conferences, I often run into people who, when asked what their book is about, say things like, "It's a book about animal rights," "It's about a group of teens that learn how bad pre-marital sex is," "I'm writing about a girl who learns that teachers make huge sacrifices for their students," "I'm writing to teach the consequences of lying."

These could all be considered worthy themes for novels, but when a writer comes at a story with a plan to lecture or "teach," the book is preachy before any word has been written.

And a book doesn't have to be about religion to be preachy.

Does this mean you can never have a theme in mind when you start a book? Of course you can, but I would advise that you be on your guard against skewing the story toward your point of view. Every author has a worldview, beliefs that unintentionally come through the story and characters. A good author should always strive to hide her own voice and opinions and be true to her characters' beliefs. But this is very difficult to do.

When writing a book proposal, I always state my intended

theme. I base this theme on what I'm hoping my main character will learn on his journey. And this is the big difference, I think. A story takes a character on a personal journey where he faces fears and grows because of it. But with a forced theme, the author will do all she can to make it fit, even if it doesn't match the characters.

So how do you portray the theme using your characters and their beliefs? Here are some ideas that have worked in other books:

Your character believes in a lie.

In *Matched* by Ally Condie, Cassia trusts The Society to make the right choices and protect the people. She learns over the course of the book that The Society is lying, and she has to decide if she wants to continue to live a lie or if freedom is worth the fight. The theme of *Matched* is freedom. Freedom to make your own choices, freedom of speech, freedom to remember.

The lie in *Matched* is something everyone believes. But characters often believe lies that are personal, and these can turn into great themes. Your character might believe she's ugly, unloved, a bad person because of something that happened years ago, a burden to her parents, better than everyone else, the right girl for her best friend's boyfriend, entitled to steal things, unworthy of an education.

A bad habit.

A bad habit might be a gateway to a theme. In *Fablehaven*, Seth is a rule breaker. One of the themes in *Fablehaven* is that obedience can protect you. Seth learns that the hard way when the angry fairies turn him into a blobby beast after he breaks the rules.

The story requires something noble of your character

Sometimes the plot of your novel asks something of your character. In my Blood of Kings trilogy, Achan learns that a good king must sacrifice, that a king's hopes and dreams and wants are not as important when it comes to his people. Sacrifice is an overall theme of that series.

Whatever theme you wind up exploring in your manuscript, I advise you to portray the opposite point of view in an equal and fair manner. In *The Perfect Match* by Jodi Picoult, Nina is a trial lawyer who prosecutes child molesters. While she recognizes the bad parts of the system—criminals sometimes walk free—she also believes in the system. Until it's *her* son who gets molested. Does she put her faith in the system to give him justice when she's seen it reject justice for so many children? Or does she take matters into her own hands? It's a heart-wrenching read because both courses of action pull at Nina and, because of that, they pull at the reader.

Make it Yours:

1. Write down one or two themes from your story.

2. What lie does your character believe? In what ways does that lie reinforce the theme of the book, and in what ways does it oppose the theme?

3. Does your main character have a bad habit that could play into a theme?

4. Does the plot of your story ask something of your main character? (Like in *The Perfect Match* where Nina is asked to be patient and trust the system or in The Blood of Kings trilogy where Achan is asked to sacrifice.) If not, brainstorm some ideas of how it can.

5. Try writing a scene or two with what you brainstormed and see how it feels.

But ... What If Readers Don't Like My Theme?
by Stephanie

I'm not the type of writer who plans a theme ahead of time. When I'm working on a book, the way it feels to me is that my story is wrapped around a core issue . . . but I don't know what it is yet. I have to keep drilling deeper into the characters and plot to uncover the truth inside.

Sometimes writers—especially writers who have a debut about to release—tell me they're worried about getting bad reviews, or they're worried readers won't like a particularly controversial element of their plot. It's something I get nervous about too. I'm a people pleaser, and I want people to like me. I hate reading reviews that rip apart how I handled an issue, and I won't lie and tell you I'm tough about it—I cry. And then I mope. And then, days later, I slowly ease my way back into writing.

But something I regularly have to remind myself of is that my goal is not to please everyone—thankfully, since that's impossible—but to tell the truth. And sometimes the truth is hard to stomach, and sometimes it's going to make people mad because they don't want their worldview being messed with.

Not only is it okay if readers get mad about what you have to say, it might even be a good thing. Writing a book that touches someone's heart, that speaks to them, often means you're writing something that will repel another person. Art is so subjective, and every reader will react differently.

When you take stuff from one writer, it's plagiarism; but when you take it from many writers, it's research.
—Wilson Mizner

Do Your Research

by Jill

Research not only teaches you about necessary elements for your story, it can inspire you. Stories written without the help of research often fall flat. You can research things for your story before you write a word, while you're writing that first draft, or during the editing stage to add interesting details.

If you're writing historical fiction, accurate information is very important, so you'll likely need to read many, many nonfiction books about your chosen era. But research isn't necessary only for historical writers. Sometimes you need to learn how things work in our contemporary world, and researching the topic is the only way to learn.

But where to start?

Books

When I start a new project, one of the first things I do is collect a pile of books. If I'm working on a fantasy novel, I read other fantasy books. When I'm writing dystopian, I read other dystopian books. I do this for two reasons. First, it helps me to read books in the same genre to get my mind into that particular environment of storytelling.

43

Secondly, it helps me know what's already been done so that I'll be aware of similarities in my story in time to change things.

I also read nonfiction books on related topics. When I wrote *By Darkness Hid*, I read a book called *Medieval Swordsmanship* by John Clements to help me learn sword fighting techniques. I wrote a proposal for a book about a girl in a sorority and read some nonfiction exposé books about Greek organizations. For a western steampunk idea, I read some books on Lewis and Clark's expedition and books on Native American tribes in the northwest, where my story was going to take place.

A Note from Stephanie

Some writers are adamant about not reading in the genre they're currently writing for fear of it stifling their own creativity or of unintentional "borrowing." I try to hold off on reading anything in the contemporary YA genre if I'm currently writing a first draft. It messes with my voice and fills me with doubts, so for me it's better to hold off until I'm in the editing stage.

Libraries

Unless you have an extravagant book allowance, research will put you on a first name basis with your librarian in no time.

Libraries are still excellent sources of information on all subjects. You can find books, magazine articles, and newspapers that sometimes go back hundreds of years. If the library is local to the area that you're writing about, there might also be a town history of some kind that you can look at. And keep in mind that most writers regularly use the interlibrary loan system, where you go through your library to borrow a book from a *different* library.

Online

The Internet is the most convenient tool for writers. You can find so much information in seconds. It's truly amazing. Be sure to verify any information you find online with at least one other source, especially if you're writing historical fiction.

Wikipedia- You can find almost anything on Wikipedia these days. It's not always true, so do be careful.

etymonline.com- This is a great site to look up the history of a word and find out when it was first used and whether or not your characters might say it.

Google Maps- You can look up almost any US location—and some international locations by zooming in as far as possible and dragging the little orange man onto the road. You can actually "walk" down the roads. I did this for a book I was working on. I walked all over Phoenix, Arizona and was able to describe landmarks without having to leave my Oregon home. Pretty sweet.

Google Translate- This is a great tool for helping you check the meanings of foreign words. It's not good for finding accurate language translations, though, so if it's important for your story to have foreign language, find a real translator. I found Google Translate useful when researching Russia. When I stumbled onto foreign websites, I could copy and paste the Cyrillic text into Google Translate and was able to read it. This worked for Japanese sites too.

YouTube- There are videos for almost any subject on YouTube. For my dystopian novel *Captives*, I found videos of people exploring storm drains, police officers getting shot with Tasers, firefighters setting a controlled burn, and people smoking electric cigarettes. For my Blood of Kings trilogy I watched videos on skinning birds and sword fighting. And for *The New Recruit* I looked up videos for people visiting Moscow. Invaluable.

Specialty Websites- There are millions of useful websites for the researching writer. Google "popular names from 1893" and you'll get several links. There are historical websites for all kinds of topics and countries. You can find sites on dog pedigrees, types of guns, vegetation and wildlife for different states, police procedures. Pretty much anything you could ever want. I've even found personal blogs with stories that match the topic I'm looking for.

Interviews

Finding an expert on a certain topic is better than any website. I've interviewed firemen, hunters, doctors, and scientists for the books I've written. I also wrote a book about Venezuela that wouldn't have been possible without the first-hand accounts of the girl who traveled there. She was able to answer questions about smell, foods she ate, and concerns of the people who lived in the village. I couldn't have found that online.

If you're going to interview someone, be sure and have a list of questions written up in advance. You want to be as quick and as thorough as possible without wasting too much of your interviewee's time. And always ask if you can call or email with any follow-up questions you may think of later.

Research Trip

If you're writing about a specific location, no amount of research can beat actually going to that place. When you get the opportunity to take a research trip, be sure to plan in advance. List the places you might want to visit, topics you want to investigate further, and have a list of questions you're looking to find answers for. Be friendly, introduce yourself as an author, and you'll be surprised how many people are willing to help.

Other Ideas

You can also get information from historical societies, visiting museums, and joining historical writers groups. If you're a historical writer, you might consider joining some of these groups now. Making friends with other historical writers is a very good idea because you can help each other.

Doing research and learning how to use it in your writing can make your book so much more realistic. Take the time to do it right.

46

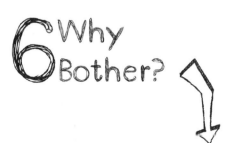

Inspiration usually comes during work, not before it.
–Madeleine L'Engle

6 Why Bother?

by Stephanie

At this point in the editing process, you might be thinking, "Is it even worth it? This book has so many problems. Should I just cut my losses and move on to a new story?"

I have totally been in that place. And I'm guessing I'll be in that place again at some point.

One of the first things I ask myself in this situation is, "Does my idea have potential to be a great book?" (Ideally you ask yourself this *before* you ever start writing, but sometimes I get too excited about an idea and rush into it.)

Of course this begs another question: What makes a book great? Here are five elements that I think are critical:

A main character in a sympathetic situation

I'll use examples from *Harry Potter and the Sorcerer's Stone* and *The Help*, which are totally different genres but both great books. Harry is an orphan being raised by a horrid family, and Skeeter is a white girl in the south in the 1960s who wants to help black maids tell their stories. Both are sympathetic to the modern reader.

47

A main character who is a hero in some way and facing an impossible situation

As a baby, Harry somehow defeated the darkest, most powerful wizard, though he's not sure how, and Skeeter is risking her life to tell an important story and promote social justice.

A unique storyworld

Hogwarts School and Mississippi in the tumultuous 1960s.

A theme or takeaway message that will impact readers

After being treated wretchedly the first eleven years of his life, Harry finds himself capable of more than he ever imagined. It makes us feel like despite whatever obstacles are in *our* lives, we too are capable of overcoming.

In *The Help*, Skeeter breaks away from cultural norms to stand up for equality for people of all races. It makes us want to do the same for social injustices that we see in our society.

A great ending

Well, I don't want to spoil anything for anyone who hasn't yet enjoyed the Harry Potter series or *The Help*, but the endings pack a punch.

Can a book be successful without these elements? Definitely. *Gossip Girl* doesn't have a heroic main character or a noble theme, but it's still an engrossing read and addictive series. The unique storyworld (a peek at the life of unbelievably rich and spoiled teenagers from old money families in NYC) makes up for a lot.

If you're wanting to trash your story, I'd recommend putting it away for a period of time. A month or so. Either work on another project you're feeling excited about, or take a break from writing in general. After you've gotten some space, pull the manuscript back out and read through it. When I've done this, I've had times where I think, "Yep. This is just as horrible as I thought." And I put it away again, often forever.

But other times I've thought, "You know . . . this isn't so bad. It's kinda good, actually. Maybe if I added this or that, it could work."

And when I do that, I'm often signing up for:

Book surgery

When I was working on the manuscript that evolved into *Me, Just Different*, I kept getting the same negative feedback from agents and contest judges—Skylar, my main character, was unlikeable. One agent wrote, "I don't like your main character. At all. I found her really annoying, actually."

For a few weeks, I indulged in inner protests that Skylar was *supposed* to be unlikable, that if the story was going to be about her reinventing herself, she had to start as someone who *needed reinvention*. But the evidence had piled up against me—she was a pain in the butt and no one wanted to spend time with her.

I shelved the manuscript, figuring I'd cut my losses and move on with other easier-to-like main characters.

But Skylar wouldn't let go of me.

Despite her pain in the butt qualities (or maybe because of them), I missed her. What I needed was a way to drum up some sympathy for her. Skylar needed a deeper reason for being aloof around boys . . . but also a reason to start dating her boyfriend, Eli. What I landed on was a near date rape, from which she was rescued by Eli.

I figured I'd open the story with the morning after the almost-date-rape, and then I could proceed with the story as planned. Just a 500-word scene addition, and I'd be good to go!

Um, not quite. It seems incredibly obvious to me now that you can't casually toss in a character barely escaping date rape, but it wasn't obvious until I rewrote my opening scene, slapped it in the front of the manuscript . . . and admitted that book surgery was required.

Book surgery means you are doing something *major* to your manuscript. Not just beefing up a plot line or fleshing out sensory details, but stuff that affects the story as a whole. To seamlessly weave in the new stuff, you'll have to look at every scene and reconsider it. Ask yourself—when I factor in the new plot thread or new character, would *this* still happen? Would the characters still feel and interact this way?

I've found the easiest way for me to do this is to write out a sentence or two for each current scene in the book on the same color of index cards. Just enough to jog my memory of what's happening: *Skylar finds out that Abbie is pregnant; Connor overhears the discussion.*

I post all the index cards in chronological order on a bulletin board. Then I take a new color of index cards and write out scenes that I know will need to be added. Again, I just jot down as much information as I need to remember my idea for the scene: *Skylar tells Connor what happened the night of Jodi's party, and Connor now realizes why she dated Eli.*

Then I take those index cards and tack them up where I think they'll fit into the story. Sometimes in this process, I discover original scenes that will need to be cut, so I put an X through them. Or sometimes I'll see a scene that needs heavy revisions. Typically I write revision ideas on a Post-it and stick it to the card.

The index cards not only help me clarify the work ahead, they give me a tool to turn to when the book surgery feels overwhelming.

Sadly, scenes and plot lines that you love will have to die to make room for material that serves the new story. About a year ago, I was doing book surgery on *The Revised Life of Ellie Sweet* and the ending was really giving me troubles. In the original manuscript, the book ended with Ellie moving to Kansas, but in the revised version, the book *also* ended with a triumph in her writing life.

I worked and worked to make everything fit, and one night it dawned on me that my endings were competing with each other. The story felt cluttered with both events happening at the end. Even though I loved the original ending, it had to die in order for the new story to work.

How do you know when book surgery is worth it or when you should scrap a project? With those completed manuscripts that I put away when I realized they needed serious surgery, I've never felt a longing to pull them back out. But Skylar had been in my "Retired Manuscripts" folder for about a month, and I was still thinking about her. I knew then that the extra work was worth it.

Since you're the one who has to do the hard work, only you can make that decision.

Make Your Good Book GREAT
The Micro Edit—Cleaning Up the Writing

A note from Stephanie on
the sheer awesomeness of the micro edit

The micro edit can make you want to pull out your hair . . . but it's also the time when your manuscript *really* starts to shine. By the end of this edit, you'll have a manuscript that's "clean as a sparkle" as my 5-year-old says.

For a lot of new writers, these nitty-gritty things like POV or active writing can cause grumbling like, "Do readers *really* care?"

They do, they just don't always know how to explain it. My husband will sometimes say, "There's something wrong with this book; I just don't know what it is."

In my book club we read Kristen Heitzmann's wonderful *Edge of Recall*. Kristen is a master of deep POV, but none of the ladies in the group knew that. Yet one of them said, "The amazing thing in this book is I feel like I deeply understand every character." Even non-writer readers could tell how flawlessly POV had been done, they just didn't know to phrase it that way.

Many of the issues you address in a micro edit are like the mortar that holds together a brick wall. Your well-crafted characters and interesting settings and plot twists are the bricks, and the time you take in the micro edit to freshen up your writing and weave in your descriptions are what keep the bricks together.

Nobody but dorky writers will admire how few adverbs you used, just like nobody admires the mortar in a brick wall, but the reader will still be able to tell what a fine craftsman you are and how easy your books are to read.

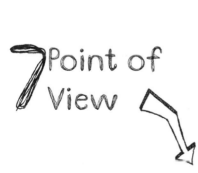

You never really understand a person until you consider things from his point of view. –Harper Lee

Point of View

Point of View Basics
by Jill

Point of view is a tricky thing to learn, but once you grasp it, you'll be able to pull the reader into your character's world so far that the *reader* becomes your main character. That's one attribute of a great storyteller.

Point of view is the perspective of the story. There are four perspectives a story can be written in and each has a different level of narrative distance, which is the feeling of closeness between the point of view character(s) and the reader.

Once you choose a point of view perspective, you must decide if the story will be written in past tense or present tense. Past tense reads like is has already happened. Present tense reads like it's happening right now. Most stories are written in first person past tense or third person past tense. First person present tense is, at *present*, a popular choice as well.

When you write a story, pick one point of view, one tense, and stick with them. There are some novels that mix it up a bit (*The Help* by Katherine Stockett comes to mind) but that's tougher than it looks, so if this is your first novel or if you're early in your writing journey, be cautious as you walk this path.

Let's cover the four perspectives:

Omniscient Point of View

In omniscient points of view, God or an all-seeing narrator tells the story. It's mostly told from a third person perspective, but the God-narrator knows all, sees all, and can communicate to the reader the thoughts of different characters in the book.

The degree of knowledge that the narrator has determines his level of omniscience. If he knows what every character is thinking, then he's fully omniscient. If the narrator only reveals what certain characters are thinking, he has limited omniscience.

Omniscient point of view stretches the narrative distance between the reader and the characters by bouncing from head to head. Full omniscient perspectives are not as popular in modern fiction.

The biggest problem with omniscient points of view is that if they aren't written well, they're very confusing. Jumping from one person's head to another in the same paragraph makes it difficult for your reader to connect emotionally to the story. Omniscient is the most difficult point of view to master. I highly recommend learning how to write a single point of view before you attempt omniscience.

Here's an example of omniscient third person from the novel *Magyk* by Angie Sage. Notice how we start in Marcia's head, then move to Sarah's head, back to Marcia's, and end up in Silas's head.

Marcia looked around her. It was true, it was not somewhere you would ever expect to find a princess. In fact, Marcia had never seen such a mess before in her entire life.

In the middle of the chaos, by the newly lit fire, stood Sarah Heap. Sarah had been cooking porridge for the birthday breakfast when Marcia had pushed her way into her home, and into her life. Now she stood transfixed, holding the porridge pan in midair and staring at Marcia. Something in her gaze told Marcia that Sarah knew what was coming. This, thought Marcia, is not going to be easy. She decided to dump the tough act and start over again.

"May I sit down, please, Silas . . . Sarah?" she asked.

Sarah nodded. Silas scowled. Neither spoke.

Silas glanced at Sarah. She was sitting down, white-faced and trembling and gathering the birthday girl up onto her lap, holding her closely. Silas wished more than anything that Marcia would go away and leave them all alone, but he knew they had to hear what she had come to say. He sighed heavily and said, "Niko, give Marcia a chair."

Many classics are done in an omniscient style, but if you want to pull it off for the modern reader, I suggest you study some popular, modern books that have omniscient narrators.

Examples of popular books done in omniscient POV: the Gossip Girl series, the Septimus Heap books, the Luxe series, the Redwall series.

First person Point of View

This perspective uses "I" for the point of view character. First person is a great point of view to consider if you want to really get deep with your main character. Here's an example of first person past tense from *Out with the In Crowd* by Stephanie Morrill:

All winter break, I'd planned for this moment, the one about to happen.

"Hey," Eli said as we passed each other in the hall.

I intended to say hello back, to smile like things between us hadn't changed, but something inside me bristled. I locked my jaw, turned away from his hypnotic smile, and picked up the pace.

Then I mentally kicked my butt as I sped toward my locker. That was *not* how it should've gone.

And here's an example of first person present tense in Libba Bray's *A Great and Terrible Beauty*:

"Lily Trimble is quite beautiful, isn't she?" I say by way of trying to make pleasant small talk with Ton, a seemingly impossible task.

"An actress," Tom sneers. "What sort of way is that for a woman to live, without a solid home, husband, children? Running about like she's her own lord and master. She'll certainly never be accepted in society as a proper lady."

And that's what comes of small talk.

Part of me wants to give Tom a swift kick for his arrogance. I'm afraid to say that another part of me is dying to know what men look for in a woman. My brother might be pompous, but he knows certain things that could prove useful to me.

The frustration of writing in first person POV is that you're typically telling the story from *that* point of view the entire book. Not always. *The Help* is all in first person, but the narrators alternate. Same with *Poisonwood Bible* by Barbara Kingsolver, both of which are modern day literature triumphs.

But for a book with one first person POV, you have the wonderfulness of knowing the main character intimately, but you can have a tough time gaining perspective from other characters without it seeming forced, though Libba Gray had little trouble showing the reader what Tom was like based on his dialogue alone.

Examples of books written in first person: All Sarah Dessen novels, the Twilight saga by Stephenie Meyer, *Divergent* by Veronica Roth, the Matched Series by Ally Condie, the Delirium series by Lauren Oliver, the Percy Jackson novels by Rick Riordan.

Second Person Point of View

This perspective uses "you" for the point of view character. This is a really rare style of storytelling, most often used in choose-your-own-adventure novels. Here's an example of second person past tense from *The Abominable Snowman* by R. A. Montgomery.

You are a mountain climber. Three years ago you spent the summer at a climbing school in the mountains of Colorado. Your instructors said that you had natural skills as a climber. You made rapid progress, and by the end of the summer you were leading difficult rock and ice climbs.

That summer, you became close friends with a boy named Carlos. The two of you made a good climbing team. Last year you and he were chosen to join an international team. The expedition made it to the top of two unclimbed peaks in South America.

One night on that expedition, the group was seated around the cook tent at the base camp. The expedition leader, Franz, told stories of climbing in the Himalayas, the highest mountains in the world.

"The Yeti is said to be a huge beast," Franz tells you, "perhaps a cross between a gorilla and a human. People cannot agree what it is."

"Is the Yeti dangerous?" Carlos asked.

Franz shrugged. "Some say it is. Other people say the Yeti is very gentle."

"Have you ever seen one?" you inquire.

The pitfalls of this POV are obvious. It's tricky to sustain over an entire story, and it can be pretty distracting for the reader.

Examples: We could only come up with a couple books that have sections written in second person. *The Girls' Guide to Hunting and Fishing* by Melissa Bank has a chapter in second, *Cherry* by Mary Karr is a memoir partially written in second, and *Hart's Hope* by Orson Scott Card has sections written in second as well.

Third Person Point of View

This perspective uses the character's name or "he" or "she" for the point of view character. Here's an example of third person past tense from *The Maze Runner* by James Dashner:

"You know this girl, shank?" Alby asked, sounding ticked off.

Thomas was shocked by the question. *"Know* her? Of course I

59

don't know her. I don't know anyone. Except you guys."

"That's not . . ." Alby began, then stopped with a frustrated sigh. "I meant does she look *familiar* at all? Any kind of feelin' you've seen her before?"

"No. Nothing." Thomas shifted, looked down as his feet, then back at the girl.

Alby's forehead creased. "You're sure?" He looked like he didn't believe a word Thomas said, seemed almost angry.

What could he possibly think I have to do with this? Thomas thought. He met Alby's glare evenly and answered the only way he knew how. "*Yes.* Why?

Once you've chosen your narrative style, you also must decide whether to use a single point of view or multiple points of view. A single POV means that you will stick with one character's POV for the whole story, like James Dashner did with *The Maze Runner*. The reader never sees the story from another perspective. In multiple points of view, the story could be told from many perspectives, one at a time.

The Sisterhood of the Traveling Pants is a good example of multiple points of view. There are four POV characters, and each character has her own chapters, though in each of the four books, a different girl gets her turn being the main character.

Examples: There are tons! I mentioned two in this section— *Uglies* by Scott Westerfield and The Sisterhood of the Travelling Pants books by Ann Brashares. *Edge of Recall* by Kristen Heitzmann, *Incarceron* by Catherine Fisher, *The Time Traveler's Wife* by Audrey Niffenegger.

Tightening Point of View

If you're trying to write a deep point of view, work hard to get your writing as close as possible to your point of view characters. This means to use only one point of view at a time. Some things to watch for as you edit are:

1. Don't tell us anything the character doesn't know.

Say you write, "Little did Shelley know, the monster was right behind her."

In deep point of view, if Shelley doesn't know that the monster is right behind her, then the reader can't know either. Not only does this sentence break deep point of view, but it's a nasty bit of telling. You spoiled the whole story by telling the reader about the monster! Try instead, "Shelley's gut tightened at the rank smell of rotten fish that came in a humid gust at the back of her neck. The hairs on her arms danced. Something was behind her!"

That's Shelley's point of view. She senses that something is behind her but doesn't know for certain until she turns around. And this way the readers experience what she's feeling, hearing, seeing, tasting, smelling, and sensing. They experience her fear.

2. Don't jump into someone else's thoughts.

It doesn't work in real life, and unless you're writing omniscient or about a telepathic character, it doesn't work in fiction. For example:

> Kate glared at Edward. What a pain little brothers were! Why did he get away with taking her stuff all the time? Maybe she could ship him off to Australia media mail. That would teach him.
>
> If Kate wouldn't always boss him, he'd behave more. Edward really only wanted his sister to play with him. The other kids in third grade didn't have a big sister as cool as her, but she always yelled at him. He almost cried the last time, which was totally wimpy, but at least she was paying some attention to him, even if it was yelling.
>
> Mr. Jones always took his son's side. How could he not? Kate was careening through some bizarre teenage girl phase beyond his understanding. She constantly tortured the family, especially Edward. As a good father should, he stepped in, but Kate always took it as a personal attack.

The switches in POV in that example are confusing. Most readers want to follow one character at a time. They don't want a new one every two sentences. It's hard for them to know which one to invest in, which brings us to:

3. One at a time, please.

If you want to write multiple points of view, you can. Just do one at a time. That is, one per scene or one per chapter. With the example above, I'd rewrite this section to come from Kate's point of view. If I wanted the reader to know how Edward and Mr. Jones felt, I could use dialogue to get it said. They could all have a big fight, or Mr. Jones could come up to his daughter's room and try to talk some sense into her.

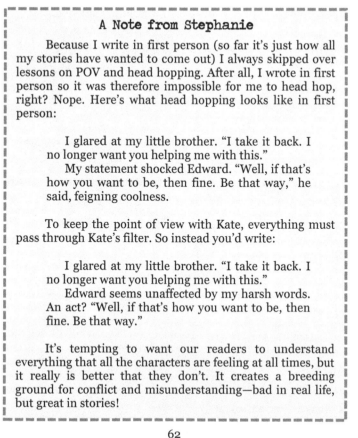

A Note from Stephanie

Because I write in first person (so far it's just how all my stories have wanted to come out) I always skipped over lessons on POV and head hopping. After all, I wrote in first person so it was therefore impossible for me to head hop, right? Nope. Here's what head hopping looks like in first person:

I glared at my little brother. "I take it back. I no longer want you helping me with this."
My statement shocked Edward. "Well, if that's how you want to be, then fine. Be that way," he said, feigning coolness.

To keep the point of view with Kate, everything must pass through Kate's filter. So instead you'd write:

I glared at my little brother. "I take it back. I no longer want you helping me with this."
Edward seems unaffected by my harsh words. An act? "Well, if that's how you want to be, then fine. Be that way."

It's tempting to want our readers to understand everything that all the characters are feeling at all times, but it really is better that they don't. It creates a breeding ground for conflict and misunderstanding—bad in real life, but great in stories!

Make it Yours:
1. Pick a scene from your book that involves more than one character. Try writing the scene from a different character's point of view. How does it feel? What did the new character describe that the original character didn't? Were there things the new character didn't even notice? What does the new character hear the original POV character say? Is it what your original POV character intended?

2. Now take a look at the scene as you originally wrote it—are there any changes you want to make?

Giving Your Narrative a Boost

In any story you need an even mix of narrative, action, and dialogue, but I've read a lot of manuscripts that don't have enough narrative from the point of view character.

Narrative is the stream of consciousness that passes through your character's mind to depict his feelings and thoughts. It's his inner monologue. Not the italicized thoughts. Those are treated more like dialogue. (We'll get to italicized thoughts in Chapter 14.)

Here's an example of narrative thoughts from *The Amulet of Samarkand* by Jonathan Stroud. The point of view character here is Bartimaeus, a very snarky demon.

At last it looked as if the urchin was plucking up the courage to speak. I guessed this by a stammering about his lips that didn't seem to be induced by pure fear alone. I let the blue fire die away, to be replaced by a foul smell.

The kid spoke. Very squeakily.

"I charge you . . . to . . . to . . ." Get on with it! "T-t-tell me your n-name."

That's usually how they start, the young ones. Meaningless waffle. He knew, and I knew that he knew, my name already;

otherwise how could he have summoned me in the first place? You need the right words, the right actions, and most of all the right name. I mean, it's not like hailing a cab—you don't get just *anybody* when you call.

I chose a rich, deep, dark chocolaty sort of voice, the kind that resounds from everywhere and nowhere and makes the hairs stand up on the back on inexperienced necks.

"Bartimaeus."

Narrative thought can also be used in between dialogue. Here's an example from my book *The New Recruit*. Spencer is a sarcastic fifteen-year-old.

Outside, dawn had lit the campus in pale light but not enough to raise the temperature. I poured on the speed, hoping to ditch Arianna.

Unfortunately, she jogged to keep up. "How long did you use the broom before you realized it was a prank?" she asked.

"Not long."

"Isn't this neat? I hoped I'd get called. I speak three languages already, but that doesn't guarantee—"

"How come you wear those weird skirts?" I asked, hoping rudeness might shut her up.

"You like them?" Arianna said, glancing down at her skirt. "I think our uniforms skirts are immodest, so I—"

"They go to the knee," I said. As did our cheerleaders' skirts, unfortunately.

"Exactly," Arianna said. "So I petitioned to get rid of them. Mr. McKaffey turned me down but said I could wear a longer skirt if I wanted to, as long as it was navy blue. So I sewed up a dozen different styles. This one is my favorite."

"Wow." And I meant it.

"Every year I ask God to give me a word, and this year he gave me the word *service*. And now this opportunity has come! It's such a God thing."

Arianna dove into an oration on being a servant of God, as if that would somehow make me want to be one too. Weird strategy. I ignored her babbling while zigzagging through the mob. I turned down the freshman hallway, which was filled with rowdy students and clanging lockers.

Arianna stopped off at her locker. "See you in homeroom."

That settled that. I'd skip homeroom for the rest of the year if only to avoid any more heart-to-hearts with Mission-Ari Sloan.

As you can see from both of those examples, narrative thoughts help the reader get to know the point of view character. Because the reader is privy to his inmost thoughts, the reader feels as though he is Bartimaeus or Spencer.

And that's the goal of writing a great point of view.

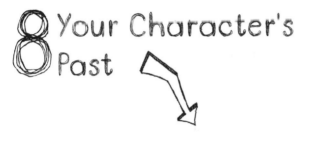

I try to leave out the parts that people skip.
–Elmore Leonard

8 Your Character's Past

Flashbacks
by Stephanie

One of the toughest things for me to overcome as a writer was my desire to explain everything to the reader. Because I had invested so much time thinking up these characters and their histories, I wanted the reader to "get" them right away. And because of that I loaded down my stories with flashbacks and backstory.

Flashbacks are scenes where the writer cuts away from the current action to transport the reader to something that happened in the past. It's like when Harry Potter fell into Dumbledore's pensieve—that kind of feeling.

Backstory is the explanations that get littered throughout your story. They feel more like a whispered aside to the reader. *Hey, Jenna is acting this way because Dylan dumped her last week.*

Backstory isn't bad writing, but it gets a bad rep because it often gets used clumsily. I certainly fumbled with it in my early writing days. This is a snippet from a high school manuscript of mine. I've bolded the part that's backstory:

This day was different, however. Today she stood in the doorway a stranger to them all. **At the end of freshman year, Paige had tearfully moved away from Brawder, California to some unknown town in Missouri, and no one had heard a word from her.** Now here she was, a year later, on the first day of junior year.

This paragraph happens on the first page of the story. While eventually, yes, the readers need to know what happened to Paige, they don't need to know right away. The beginning of a story is a time for planting questions, which is what I did with "today she stood in the doorway a stranger to them all." Since the readers have just learned that the other students know Paige already, they're (ideally) intrigued by why today is different, why she's a stranger.

Planting questions is great—answering them in the next sentence is not.

If the readers don't need the information in order to understand what's happening, then it's not the right time to hand it over.

But of course your story would be confusing and your characters flat if you didn't weave in backstory. I think the key to making those sentences interesting is they should come through the filter of the POV (point of view) character.

Here's an example. Again, I've bolded the backstory:

"I think you guys should just be friends," Meghan says to me.

Of course. **Ever since Joel stomped on her heart last spring, Meghan has been all about being "just friends" with boys.**

I dry the counter with a towel. "You know, you don't always have a choice in the matter."

Much better, right? In that story of mine from high school, the backstory sentence felt more like Stephanie-the-author was explaining to you what was unusual about Paige being at school. But in this one, it feels like the POV character is telling you why Meghan is behaving the way she is.

It tells us everything we need to know at that moment. Which is that Meghan's advice is tainted by her experiences. We don't need an additional paragraph explaining what exactly happened between Meghan and Joel and whose fault it was. Maybe we'll need that later, but not yet.

But sometimes a sentence or two, or even a paragraph of explanation, doesn't capture the emotion of the character's past. And that's when you might consider a flashback instead.

Because flashbacks cut away from the forward progress of your plot, they should be chosen wisely.

When to use a flashback

• This is a moment in time that has forever altered your character.
• You've spent time in the story building up tension about what happened on "that night" or "that afternoon" and your flashback reveals what went down.

When not to use a flashback

• You wrote the scene, but then your timeline changed, but you really want to put it somewhere . . .
• It's a cute scene and you love it and you think readers will find it a fun bunny trail. (I was totally guilty of this as a new writer. Flashbacks are not about fun, but about revealing something deeper.)

Sometimes flashbacks are used in prologues, which I'm not a fan of. Typically, the reader doesn't have enough information about the characters for the flashback to have the emotional punch it might have later in the story. With that being said, *The Apothecary's Daughter* is one of my favorite books, and Julie Klassen opens with a flashback prologue. So it can be effective in the hands of a skilled writer.

As a general guideline, I would suggest only one or maybe two flashbacks per story.

In the Skylar Hoyt books, before the first book opens, she's nearly date raped at a party. This is, obviously, a very important turning point in Skylar's life. It's also not really something she likes to think about, and because she's pushing the pain away, there's no need to flashback to the scene in book one, *Me, Just Different.* Or in the second book, *Out with the In Crowd.* It isn't until halfway through book three, *So Over It,* that we find out what happened that night, and then the scene is given almost an entire chapter.

But by now, the reader has gone through two and a half books of not knowing exactly what happened that night (Skylar's also a little fuzzy on the details, as it turns out). By the time the readers reach the flashback, they understand the significance of it. Whereas if I'd put the scene in the first book, or if I'd opened Skylar's story with it, the way I'd considered, the reader wouldn't have understood as deeply.

You don't need to strip all the backstory and flashback scenes from your novel, but hunt them down and assess the pacing and their contribution.

Some people have a way with words, and other people . . . oh, uh, not have way.
—Steve Martin

9 Dialogue That Speaks

by Stephanie

Is there anything better than well-crafted dialogue? It's my favorite part of reading and writing, and if it's off, the whole story can feel flat or forced to me. While I can't always picture my characters the way some writers can, by the end of the first draft, I can *always* hear them—the tenor of the voice, their stutters, their unique way of stringing sentences together.

You have two nuts and bolts type tools when you're writing dialogue—word choice and punctuation.

Punctuation

We can all agree that these three sentences have the same words but mean completely different things:

"Grandma always made pumpkin pie."

"Grandma always made pumpkin pie!"

"Grandma always made pumpkin pie?"

Or maybe your character trails off or makes an aside comment:

"Grandma always made pumpkin pie . . ." (Or you can make a trailing off question, "Grandma always made pumpkin pie . . . ?")

Or maybe your character doesn't even get all his words out. For a character who's interrupted, you want to use the em-dash:

"Grandma always made pump—"

Be purposeful with your punctuation. What I see overused the most is the exclamation point. Those you'll want to really examine. If you're unsure at all, I would try going without. Some publishing professionals even say they only like to see one exclamation point per *book*.

You can use punctuation to show your pauses as well. Here's one with an ellipses:

"Grandma always made pumpkin pie."
"So maybe we should make one too . . . to honor her."

I'm also rather fond of em-dashes for pauses. *The Chicago Manual of Style* instructs it be formatted this way:

"Grandma always made pumpkin pie. And so today"—I take Joel's hand in my own—"that's what we're gonna do."

But I've seen variations of this format in published novels. Until a publisher tells you to do otherwise, sticking with *The Chicago Manual of Style* is a safe call.

I like how the em-dashes give the reader a glimpse of corresponding action. And I like that about using an action beat or character's thoughts to indicate a pause or hesitation:

"Grandma always made pumpkin pie."
Joel blinked a couple times. "She did?"

"Grandma always made pumpkin pie." **How could I say this to him? He was gonna be crushed.** "But today we're having pecan."

Maybe grammar isn't your thing—it's not mine either—but punctuation helps you communicate your words clearly. It's like if you were giving a speech, and your words were beautiful and your message great, but your microphone kept cutting out or making your voice sound weird. Your listeners would be distracted even if the speech was brilliant. The same is true with your dialogue. Like a microphone, punctuation will help pass your message along clearly, and it shouldn't call much attention to itself.

The Word Choice

Let's turn our attention from punctuation to the actual words being used in your sentences.

In an early manuscript of mine, one of my teenage boy characters kept using the word "fabulous." Everything was fabulous—weather, clothes, classes. But no straight guy says fabulous that often. I don't think my husband has *ever* used that word.

While a character's backstory isn't a "nut and bolt tool" for your dialogue, it's a support beam for your word choice. Where's the character from? How educated is he? How educated were his *parents*? Applying a character's backstory to the way he speaks is the key to creating character voices that differentiate from each other.

In *The Revised Life of Ellie Sweet,* my main character Ellie is sixteen, but because she's an aspiring novelist, I have her using bigger words and *who* and *whom* correctly. But her friend Chase was raised by parents who speak broken English, and he's pretty rough around the edges. Where Ellie might say, "My parents don't traditionally buy me presents for Valentine's Day," Chase would say, "My parents don't get me nothing."

Make it Yours:

List ten or so of your characters on the left side of your paper. Across the top of your paper, write several items or phrases that people say differently. I've selected a soft drink, purse, bathroom, and what they say when they say in a moment of surprise or disbelief. Then make a list of what each might say.

Here's an example:

	Soft Drink	Purse	Bathroom	Surprise/ Disbelief
John	Pop	Bag	Toilet	Really?
Sally	Soda	Handbag	Restroom	No way.
Lucy	Coke	Purse	The necessary	You're kidding me.

What's your problem?

Another way to keep your characters' voices from running together is to give them their own problem instead of letting their world revolve around the main character. (I also talk about this in the cast of characters section.) In my early drafts, conversations all hinged on my main character—her problems, her needs, her issues.

When your main character is interacting with other characters, be sure those other characters have their own thoughts and lives going on. If your main character wants to talk all nostalgic-like about Grandma's pumpkin pie, then have the other person wanting pecan pie. Or have him bring up the Thanksgiving where everyone fought, and he finished the day scraping pumpkin pie off the ceiling. Or he can bring up how Grandma never made pumpkin pie when *he* came to visit . . .

When you allow the other characters to have their own thoughts and problems, dialogue instantly becomes more interesting.

"Grandma always made pumpkin pie."
"Maybe for *you* she did."

Or:

"Grandma always made pumpkin pie."
"I know—but her pecan pie was so much better."

While you want your dialogue to have a real-life quality to it, you don't want it to read like a real-life conversation. Because that would be bo-ring. Alfred Hitchcock said that a good story was, "life, with the dull parts taken out." Apply this to dialogue too. At a real-life Thanksgiving dinner, you'll get cornered by Aunt Trudy and she'll talk to you for twenty minutes about Grandma's pumpkin pie and how she actually grated fresh nutmeg and always picked her pumpkins from so-and-so's pumpkin patch.

Don't make your readers sit through long monologues or pleasantries. ("Hi, how are you?" "Good, how are you?") Occasionally it might work for the story, like an awkward moment when two people who broke up last week are seeing each other for the first time, but in general "Hi, how are you?" discussions can all be nixed.

Make it Yours:

Pick a conversation in your manuscript at random. What was the non-POV character thinking about before the POV character started talking to him? Is that coming through in the dialogue? How would the dialogue change if the non-POV character had been thinking about something completely different?

The Strategy

A problem I often see in dialogue is characters that employ no strategy in how they deliver information.

My husband and I have been a couple for half our lives now, since we were freshman in high school, yet still when I come to him with news, there's strategy involved. I'm not talking about me trying to manipulate him into doing something, I mean *any* news I share. News that will make him happy I share in a different way than news that will upset him. How will this affect him? When would be the best time to share it?

And this is a man who I'm confident isn't going to leave me, no matter what I say to him. Real life conversation involves strategy, and story world conversation should too.

Of course it can be a lot of fun to toss in a character who tends to say whatever pops into his brain, but how often do you say everything you're thinking?

When you're put on hold for ten minutes and someone finally comes back on the line and says, "I'm so sorry for the wait," what's your answer? I always say, "Don't worry about it," even though I've spent the last nine-and-a-half minutes grumbling snarky comments like, "Don't worry—my time isn't important. I'm not spending precious kid-free minutes trying to sort out this stupid billing error that's *your* fault. Take your sweet time."

Make it Yours:

Find a conversation in your manuscript in which one character is delivering information to another character. Does he have a strategy? If so, what is it? Why is he sharing this particular information right now? What if he had another motive? Fear, anger, jealousy, hope, love. How would that change the flavor of the conversation?

T.M.I.

Sometimes writers try to work information into dialogue that should *not* be in there. One of my new writing pet peeves is an exchange that looks like this:

"Sally, how long have we known each other?"
"For ten years."
"That's why I'm giving you this ten-carat diamond."

I've seen variations of this on TV, in books, and in movies. Makes me crazy! Because that's not the kind of thing we say to each other. I never turn to my husband with moony eyes and say, "Honey, how long have we been married?" Not only is it information we both know, it's information we both know that we both know.

Now, I might say, "I can't believe we've been married for eight years," or, "I can't believe you've put up with me for eight years," but I've yet to say to him, "How long have we been married?"

I often see this kind of info dumping with dates and timeframes. Like, "Since today is Wednesday, do you have that report for me?" Or like this little gem from one of my early manuscripts:

"My father . . . is being transferred at the end of June."
"The end of June?! We're a week into June already!"

How forced is *that*? Sheesh. It's much more natural, I think, if the response is, "That's, like, three weeks away!"

Dialogue has to be natural. Read it out loud and ask yourself honestly if people would talk about things in such a way. If they wouldn't, find another way to get the info into the story.

Group Conversations

Of course not all your conversations are going to be between two people. Often times you have a big group of characters engaging with each other. While necessary, it can really drag down the pacing.

A strategy for handling those is using sub-conversations. Say you're at a dinner party, seated at a long table. Rarely does everyone at the table engage in the same conversation. Typically you talk to whoever is across from you or next to you. You might catch snippets of other conversations, but mostly you interact with those closest.

That means as a writer, you want to be strategic with where characters are positioned in the conversation, because those are the characters your point of view character will be interacting with. You want to optimize the tension.

I wrote a scene awhile back in which my main character found herself on a triple date. As soon as I wrote myself into this situation, I wanted to write my character out of there because the pacing was so tricky.

There are six characters in this conversation. My main character, Sabrina, is there because her best friend Autumn likes Patrick and wants to go on this group date with him. But what Autumn doesn't know is that Patrick asked Sabrina out the day before and she turned him down. So to optimize the tension, Sabrina needed to be by Patrick and Autumn.

Then I also needed to fill out the lunch since it's supposed to be a group date. Sabrina's other best friend, Izzy, is there, plus two of Patrick's friends, whom Patrick brought to "occupy" Sabrina's friends while he attempted to build something with her. Of course Autumn thinks that Patrick is *her* date, so she's rather confused on the dynamics, which makes conversation awkward and tricky.

In your manuscript, if the whole group is talking, the topic must be something that engages most or all members. Here's how part of the scene looks in my manuscript:

Nate pushes napkins to our side of the table. "You eaten here before, Autumn?"

Autumn blinks, as if confused by why he's addressing her. "Uh, no." She turns to me. Apparently she's designated *me* as Nate's date. "Have you, Sabrina?"

"A couple times." I fiddle with my queen of hearts. I don't know why this place doesn't just take your name or give you a number or something, why they insist on foisting a germy playing card on everyone.

"Their reubens are the best," Patrick says.

Izzy flicks her nine of clubs, makes it spin on the table. "Reubens are disgusting."

"Agreed." The third guy, whose name I don't remember, grins at Izzy as if they are officially soul mates. "Sauerkraut is the second grossest food on the planet. I mean, what is it?"

Patrick and I answer at the same time. "Cabbage."

Patrick flashes those white teeth and dimples at me, but I look away.

"What's the first grossest food?" Izzy asks with a hint of a smile.

"Cottage cheese." He actually shudders when he says it.

"No way," I say. "How's that possibly grosser than, say, pig's feet? Or bologna?"

Patrick is still giving me the teeth-and-dimples combo, which must be a one-two punch for girls like Autumn.

"Or soft boiled eggs?" Nate offers. "Those things freak me out."

Autumn frowns into her soda. I don't think this is the kind of conversation she imagined having on our triple quasi-date. She also probably thought she'd be sitting beside Patrick, instead of wedged between me and Izzy, with the boys on the other side of the booth. And with Patrick across from *me*.

If someone isn't contributing, you need to get him out of there. He needs to go to the bathroom or see a friend walking by. Or let him break into a side conversation with someone else. When guy number 3 and Izzy were not moving the story along, I separated them:

"I work at the AMC downtown, and Trent"—Nate jerks his thumb at Boy #3—"works at Hy-Vee."

Izzy sends her card spinning again. "When people come through your line with cottage cheese, do you shudder?"

Trent grins. "And I make them scan it themselves."

79

Izzy smiles full-on, and they lapse into their own volley of other foods that disgust them. Miracle Whip. Spam. Cheetos.

I glance at Patrick, who arches his eyebrows like *See? I knew this would work out.*

And now, because Izzy and Trent are talking, I only have four people to deal with. Soon Sabrina will receive a phone call and excuse herself.

Group conversations breathe realism into stories, but too many of them will slow down your plot. You want to cut away from them and focus on your main character as soon as you can.

Action Beats and Dialogue Tags

Action beats are a tool you can use to support your dialogue. They're like framework, really. They help you keep the pacing and the context of both your group and one-on-one conversations. You can do it with dialogue tags too, but I prefer the effect of action or thought beats.

A dialogue tag is: he said, she shouted, he yelled, she questioned. It tells the reader who's talking, and it sometimes tells the reader how the speaker is saying his dialogue, but that's all it does—*tells* us. It doesn't show us what the speaker is doing. Consider the differences:

With dialogue tags:

"Grandma always made pumpkin pie," I said tearfully.
"Sure she did," Joel retorted.

With action beats:

I wiped the tear from my cheek with my flour-dusted hands.
"Grandma always made pumpkin pie."
Joel snorted. "Sure she did."

Look at the difference that makes—we now have context and emotion. Our main character is crying, and her hands are covered in flour.

Let's view it with a thought beat thrown in now:

> I wiped the tear from my cheek with my flour-dusted hands. "Grandma always made pumpkin pie." Would I ever make one without thinking of her?

Now we don't just have context and the physical manifestation of her emotion (tears), but we have her exact thought.

When you're using action or thought beats, you want to be sure to put them in the same paragraph. Otherwise this happens:

> "Grandma always made pumpkin pie."
> I wash my hands.
> "Sure she did."
> Joel walks out of the room.

What's wrong here? You can't really tell who is saying what. It could be the narrator speaking or Joel or someone else. The reader can't know for sure and needs some clues to help him know who is saying what.

> I wash my hands. "Grandma always made pumpkin pie."
> "Sure she did." Joel walks out of the room.

Putting the narrator's action with the "Grandma always made pumpkin pie" dialogue shows the reader that "I" said those words. Putting Joel's action with the "Sure she did," shows his response.

The action tags in that example, however, are a bit generic. In first drafts, my manuscript is always filled with generic action tags. Things like: He nodded. She shrugged. She rolled her eyes. He grinned. He walked. She smiled. While your characters might shrug or gasp or shudder or smile, these things don't build tension or emotion and tend to get overused.

Keep an eye out for generic action tags and replace them with meaningful action or narrative thoughts. Try to make each tag unique and show something important about the character or the setting. For example:

> Kim clicked her long, red fingernails on the steel countertop. "I don't eat red meat."

Here we learn Kim has long, red fingernails, that the countertop is steel, that she doesn't eat red meat. Her actions and dialogue work together to show something to the reader.

When I first learned about action beats, I was amazed to see how they instantly tightened my writing, and I think you'll find the same for yours as well.

Make it Yours:

1. Do a search in your manuscript for the word "said." Do you need it? Or could you strengthen the dialogue by either showing the action or sharing the character's thought?

2. Do the same with replied, retorted, shouted, or any of your other favorite dialogue tags. Instead of telling the reader that your character shouted something in anger, could you show the anger in his words by having him throw something instead?

> Don't tell me the moon is shining; show me the glint of light on broken glass.
> —Anton Chekhov

10 Cut Out the Telling

by Jill

Someone reads your work and says, "There's too much telling here. You need to show."

Huh?

This is a great mystery for beginning writers and even for some writers who've been at it a while.

What does "telling" mean, anyway? And how do you "show?"

In some ways, I still can't explain this fully, but I can give you a great start. In fact, if you really want the best advice on this, check out Jeff Gerke's book, *The Art and Craft of Writing Christian Fiction*. Jeff uses some amazing comparisons to "show" you the difference between telling a story and showing it. Jeff says, "Toss aside your s'mores and put on your director's chapeau. It's time to stop telling stories and start making movies—on paper."

I've divided this section into four ways I see authors tell rather than show and given examples in hopes of "showing" you what I mean.

Telling the Senses

Using the five senses in your writing is great, but be careful not to "tell" the five senses. If you're using the actual words—felt, saw, heard, smelled, tasted, sensed—or other versions of these words— noticed, found, spotted, experienced, looked, watched, wondered, listened, tried, thought, etc.—you're probably telling.

Telling example: Bill felt tired.
Showing example: Bill yawned. His body ached. He hadn't slept in three days.

Telling example: Shannon spotted a bird.
Showing example: A blue jay flew across the gray sky.

Telling example: Jessie heard the tinkling of a bell.
Showing example: The bells above the entrance door tinkled.

Telling example: Angie smelled fresh bread.
Showing Example: The scent of fresh bread wafted on the breeze.

Telling example: He tasted blood.
Showing example: A metallic taste flooded his mouth.

Telling example: She sensed foreboding.
Showing example: Her skin prickled as if something was wrong.

You can't avoid every word from my list above, nor should you. And I'm not saying those words are bad. But use them carefully. Show action whenever you can rather than telling the facts. Showing gives you the opportunity to describe setting, characters, senses, and action. It helps you be specific. Every word matters. Choose wisely.

Adverbs

Adverbs that end in "ly" tend to be overused by new authors. And "ly" adverbs are *always* telling. Every once in a while it's okay to use one—I've even had editors add them to my writing!—but for the most part, cut them out. Use strong descriptive verbs to convey emotion and action rather than relying on lazy adverbs.

Poor example: "Come here," Meg said loudly.
Better example: "Come here!" Meg yelled.

Backstory in Dialogue

Flashbacks and backstory can be considered telling, and Stephanie went over that in Chapter 8. But telling backstory can also happen in dialogue. For example:

"How are you, Mike? I know you broke your leg last week. How is it feeling?"

"It's better, but I couldn't play in the basketball game last night like you did."

"I'm sorry. I know how much that means to you."

Or:

"I don't want to go to the party tonight. I'm tired of trying to meet boys," Megan said.

"But Meg, you're so pretty," Jessica said. "Your blonde curls make me jealous. And you have great posture and a nice figure. You're shorter than me, too, and I know boys like that."

My, what a "telling" way to sneak in some character description! Ha ha.

Assumptions and Interpreting Minds

Unless you're writing an omniscient point of view, you should always be inside the head of one character at a time. When you're working on your edit, watch for places where your point of view character knows something he shouldn't.

Be careful of using "seem," "I could tell," or "I knew." These words and phrases often tell the emotion of characters your POV character sees. And your point of view character can't really know how another person is feeling by interpreting the look on her face.

For example:

Meg looked at John. He seemed to think she was lying.

But Meg can't know that. She can't read John's mind. She could guess, but it's stronger to do a little more work on your rewrite. What about John's words or behavior gives Meg the impression that he thought she was lying? Did he huff and walk away? Fold his arms and scowl? Did he say, "Meg, you're full of it"? Make sure your main character isn't interpreting minds.

With a

Another signal that you might be telling is using the phrase "with a." Like in this example:

Poor: "Give up already," Dave said with a wink.
Better: Dave winked at Grace. "Give up already."

In the second example "winked" is a verb rather than a descriptor. It's stronger that way.

Make it Yours:

Do a search in your manuscript for some of the words mentioned above. You can also search for -ly words, and even for phrases like "with a." Examine the sentences you find. Are you telling? Is there a way you could be showing instead?

> Description begins in the writer's imagination, but should finish in the reader's.
> —Stephen King

11 Weaving in Description

by Jill

Editors vary on their insistence that setting and characters be described fully. Some say leave it out and let the reader imagine everything. Others say you need to paint that scene for the readers so they can see it.

I think somewhere in the middle is best.

If you describe nothing, you have what's commonly referred to as talking heads, which is a string of dialogue coming from people the reader can't see.

And if you describe too much, you keep the reader from experiencing the action of the story.

When I go back in to edit, I often find that I've described very little. If you write books on the shorter side, this is good. Going back and adding words will beef up your word count. But this is always trouble for me because I write such long books, and adding description to an already long novel is tricky.

1. Description is necessary. 2. Description is not always "telling." Description *can* be a form of telling, but that doesn't mean you can get away with describing nothing. If you don't describe the scene and characters, how will readers know what anything looks like?

Props on the Stage

Ever see a play? My son acted the part of Linus in *A Charlie Brown Christmas* last year. When we entered and took our seats, the first thing we saw was the stage, decked out for Christmas. A piano and desk with a sign that said, "Psychiatric Help 5¢," sat on one side of the stage. On the other, Snoopy's dog house had been taped to the wall, decorated with twinkle lights, and a red plastic dog dish sat on the floor in front of the blacked-out dog door. A tin can was sitting on a shelf in the background, and later, my son got to knock it down with his Linus blanket.

Everything the actors needed for the entire play was on stage from the start, waiting to be used.

You don't have to go that far.

But near the start of every scene, give the readers some sort of description. Prepare that stage. It doesn't have to be long. It simply needs to share with the reader: the location, what characters are present, and any objects that might be integral to the forthcoming scene, like the tin can for Linus to knock down or Linus's blanket.

If you plan to have a character pick up a chair and throw it later in the scene, you'd be wise to plant at least one chair in your initial description. Having a chair appear suddenly when the character needs it might be confusing to the reader if you never mentioned there were chairs in the room.

Here are a few examples of description at the start of a new scene:

> On Friday, Mr. Lynch walked around the classroom making sure everybody had written down the due date in their assignment books. Luckily, he started at the far side, giving Mitty Blake time to whisper to his best friend, "Due date for what?"
>
> —*Code Orange* by Caroline B. Cooney

So we know we're in a classroom filled with people, we know the teacher is on the other side of the room, and we know our POV character, Mitty, is sitting beside his best friend.

Here's another:

> There were six large gray tents, and each one had a black letter on it: A, B, C, D, E, or F. The first five tents were for the campers. The counselors slept in F.
>
> Stanley was assigned to D tent. Mr. Pendanski was his counselor.
>
> "My name is easy to remember," said Mr. Pendanski as he shook hands with Stanley just outside the tent. "Three easy words: pen, dance, key."
>
> —*Holes* by Louis Sachar

Here we see the layout of the camp, and we get Stanley and Mr. Pendanski's location before they start a dialogue with each other.

Let's look at one more:

> Damien leans against the warehouse. With human eyes he stares—at the burned-out church across the street, at the dark stretch of road before him, at the abandoned half-built skyscraper covering the site in shadow.
>
> —*Angel Eyes* by Shannon Dittemore

Can't you picture it? Creepy. And this description leads right into Damien's goal for the scene. Whenever you are able to combine description with action and motivation, it's a very good thing.

If we tear these examples apart, you can see that all of the scenes let the reader know where the main character is and who is with him: Mitty is sitting at a desk in a full classroom beside his friend. Stanley is standing outside a tent with Mr. Pendanski. Damien is leaning against a warehouse, alone.

Make it Yours:

Check the beginning of each scene. Have you given a description that mentions the location, what characters are present, and any important objects? If not, do so now!

Describing Through a Point of View Character

The way things are described in your story depends on which point of view character is describing them. If you're writing a female, she might point out clothing details or compare her looks to the person she's describing. A male POV might just think: She was a chick in a dress. If you're writing a male, however, he might observe a specific model of a car and know what kind of an engine it has, whereas a female might only notice that the car was old and an ugly shade of green.

Always try and bring out your point of view character's personality when you describe. Here are some examples of different ways to use description. Notice which examples characterize the POV character as well as describes something?

Narratives

As always, [Nick's] face, clothes, pose, and perfectly gelled hair looked like something from the cover of GQ magazine. He was tall and thin, but I had four inches on him.

—*The New Recruit* by Jill Williamson

Medium height, stocky build, ashy blond hair that falls in waves over his forehead. The shock of the moment is registering on his face, you can see his struggle to remain emotionless, but his blue eyes show the alarm I've seen so often in prey.

—*Hunger Games* by Suzanne Collins

Dialogue and Action Tags

"Speaking of faces, love the nose."

Tally giggled, pulling it off. "Yeah, no point in being uglier than usual."

Shay's face clouded. She wiped off an eyebrow, then looked up sharply. "You're not ugly."

92

"Oh, come on, Shay."

"No, I mean it." She reached out and touched Tally's real nose. "Your profile is great."

"Don't be weird, Shay. I'm an ugly, you're an ugly. We will be for two more weeks. It's no big deal or anything." She laughed. "You, for example, have one giant eyebrow and one tiny one."

Shay looked away, stripping off the rest of her disguise in silence.

—*Uglies* by Scott Westerfeld

"I have to go." I start up the hill again, nearly sprinting now, but again he comes after me.

"Hey. Not so fast." At the top of the hill he reaches out and puts a hand on my wrist to stop me. His touch burns, and I jerk away quickly. "Lena. Hold on a second."

Even though I know I shouldn't, I stop. It's the way he says my name: like music.

—*Delirium* by Lauren Oliver

Action

I'm saved by a Centro bus. It coughs and rumbles and spits out two old women in front of the grocery store. I climb on. Destination: The Mall.

—*Speak* by Laurie Halse Anderson

At that moment Alex struck. It was another classic Karate blow, this time twisting his body around and driving his elbow into the side of the man's head, just below the ear. The guard didn't even cry out. His eyes rolled and he went limp.

—*Stormbreaker* by Anthony Horowitz

. . . Harry was still looking out of the window, feeling increasingly nervous. Ernie didn't seem to have mastered the use of a steering wheel. The Knight Bus kept mounting the pavement, but it didn't hit anything; lines of lampposts, mailboxes, and trash cans jumped out of its way as it approached and back into position once it had passed.

—*Harry Potter and the Prisoner of Azkaban* by J. K. Rowling

Voice

There are two types of voice: author voice and character voice. An author's voice is the way he or she puts words on a page. A character's voice is how an author puts different characters' voices on the page.

I like to write character driven stories, so I strive to hide my author voice and make every word sound like that of the point of view character.

I had a lot of fun doing this in my book *Captives*. Since this book has four point of view characters, I sometimes had to describe the same thing through the eyes of different viewpoint characters. For example, three of my viewpoint characters met General Otley. And each described him differently because they're different people and don't think alike.

> Mason: One man stood out from the rest, towering over the others like some monstrous bat. His eye shade had been pushed to the top of his helmet, though a pair of sunglasses and a thick beard covered most of his face. The skin that did show was pale and flaky. He had the thin plague.
>
> Mason had only ever seen body piercings in Old movies, but this man had overdone it, in his opinion. Gold rings looped through each eyebrow and the center of his bottom lip, and a gold spike curled out of each nostril like a section of the barbed wire that topped The Safe Land walls. He had a white number eight tattooed to his cheek. His name patch said Otley.

> Levi: A third enforcer ducked through the doorway. He looked like an elk walking on its hind legs. He had dark, frizzy hair, parted down the middle, that tangled with his bushy mustache and beard. His eyes were a freakish yellow. Even weirder, two coils of gold metal shot out from each nostril like feelers on an insect. Medals and bars and fancy patches covered his uniform. The word *Otley* was embroidered on a front shirt pocket. The number eight glowed on his cheek.

Omar: . . . and Otley himself, sitting behind his desk with his beefy arms folded across his massive chest. Omar would sketch Otley as a giant boar ramming its tusks into the side of a house.

All three brothers compared General Otley to an animal, but chose different animals. Mason, a doctor, noticed his flaking skin and piercings. Levi, the leader of the Outsiders, paid more attention to Otley's beard, eyes, and metals. And Omar, an artist, thought about how he'd sketch the man to poke fun.

Each character is unique, and each voice should sound unique to that character.

Make it Yours:
Pick out three side characters from your book. Ask each of them, "How would you describe the main character?" Try writing the answers in first person, almost like a journal entry.

Description through word choice

C. S. Lewis said, "Don't use words too big for the subject. Don't say 'infinitely' when you mean 'very'; otherwise you'll have no word left when you want to talk about something really infinite."

The words you use are important in writing, but especially so in description. You want to be specific and clear to paint the best image in your reader's head.

Simple Words

In any description, always try to state where the character is in one simple and strong noun. Like: forest, bedroom, office, coast, classroom, sea. Pair the noun with descriptive verbs like: curved, stretched, crouched, stood, towered. And occasionally add adjectives like: rocky, thick, bare, crowded, grassy, colossal, and specific colors. Try to avoid "ly" adverbs.

Emotion Words

If you flip back to the examples I've given in the last few pages, notice how you can sometimes glean the character's mood from the words chosen in the description. Not all authors do this, but it's a great trick. Let's look at a couple again. I've bolded the use of words and phrases that help to evoke a certain emotion with a description.

Damien leans against the warehouse. **With human eyes he stares**—at the **burned-out** church across the street, at the **dark** stretch of road before him, at the **abandoned half-built** skyscraper covering the site in **shadow**.
—*Angel Eyes* by Shannon Dittemore

"I have to go." I start up the hill again, **nearly sprinting** now, but again he **comes after** me.
"Hey. Not so fast." At the top of the hill he **reaches out** and **puts a hand on my wrist** to stop me. **His touch burns**, and **I jerk away** quickly. "Lena. Hold on a second."
Even though **I know I shouldn't**, I stop. It's the way he says my name: like music.
—*Delirium* by Lauren Oliver

In the *Angel Eyes* example, the word choices help to evoke a creepy, dark feeling for the reader. Fear. The example from *Delirium* also evokes fear, but it's a different kind of fear, and it all changes quickly at the end of that example.

Word Pictures

Use word pictures, metaphors, and similes whenever possible because they can evoke instant mental images for the reader. A great simile or metaphor can really help a reader connect, but one that's a little too creative can jerk the reader out of the story. Make sure the ones you use work well. You can check your manuscript for similes by doing a "find" search in Microsoft Word for the word "like." Only keep the ones that flow and don't distract from the scene.

The cafeteria was at full volume when I walked in. Feeding time at the monkey house.
                                    —*Twisted* by Laurie Halse Anderson

[Arianna] was wearing a long, ruffly brown skirt with beige lace peeking out the bottom. All she needed was a parasol, and we could put her in a time machine and send her back to the Gold Rush.
                                    —*The New Recruit* by Jill Williamson

The rain came down in long knitting needles.
                                    —*National Velvet* by Enid Bagnold

The Five Senses

Always try and work the five senses into your descriptions: sight, sound, touch, taste, and smell. This is often neglected in books, and it's such an easy way to connect with the reader. You don't need to give the reader all five senses every time, but do make sure you use different ones. Try and use at least one sense per page in your novel.

The house smelled funky, like mold, bacon grease, and cigarettes. The floors were bare. Cheyenne could tell by the sound of their footsteps that they were made of wood, not tile or linoleum. She shuffled her feet so that she could hear the echo from the walls. The room sounded small.
                                    —*Girl Stolen* by April Henry

I lie in bed and listen to nine people breathing.
I have never slept in the same room as a boy before, but here I have no other option, unless I want to sleep in the hallway. Everyone else changes into the clothes the Dauntless provided for us, but I sleep in my Abnegation clothes, which still smell like soap and fresh air, like home.
                                    —*Divergent* by Veronica Roth

Make it Yours:

Pick a scene in your book, preferably one that you haven't spent much time finessing yet. Examine the words you use in your descriptions. Are they simple and descriptive? Do they convey emotion for the scene? Do they paint a word picture? How about the five senses? Have you included some? Remember, not every description needs to do all of these things, but be sure and work some of these tricks in where you can.

> All the words I use in my stories can be found in the dictionary—it's just a matter of arranging them into the right sentences.
> —W. Somerset Maugham

12 Fresh Writing

by Jill

Part of rewriting is looking at how you've put your words together and whether or not you've done that in the best way. You want to craft every sentence and paragraph so that they sweep your reader along page after page.

Seek out all things awkward, bland, repetitive, tiresome, and cliché, and work hard to make them just right.

Paragraph and Sentence Length

We live in a "get it now" generation. Everyone is in a hurry, and attention spans are short. Most readers like lots of white space. If you pick up a book and flip through it, notice the amount of text on each page compared to the amount of white space (where there's no text). You want a good balance in your manuscript. When readers flip through a book and see pages covered in text with long paragraphs and little dialogue, it looks like a lot of work to read, which doesn't look fun. Keep that in mind as you edit.

Paragraphs

Watch for super long paragraphs. They're not wrong, but if you're writing fiction that you hope will appeal to a wide variety of readers, you'll want to avoid them because readers tend to skim over long paragraphs. I recommend trying to keep paragraphs no longer than six lines in your Word document, because they'll be even longer once the text is put into book form.

Also, vary the length of your paragraphs. If you have too many really long ones, see if you can break up a few. This makes your text look more interesting to the reader and lets him know that a break is coming. And don't underestimate the power of a really short, one-sentence paragraph every now and then.

They rock.

Sentences

The same applies to the length of sentences. Too many long sentences are work for your reader. Too many short ones feel choppy, intense, and child-like. And if you write every sentence in the same structure and length, your writing will seem bland. A blend of short, medium, and long sentences with different structures is best. Below are two examples from different stages of my book *The New Recruit*. The first is an older rewrite. The second is the final version. Notice how similar the sentence lengths are in each paragraph in the first example, and how I managed to vary things in the second.

"Is that you, Spencer? This is Lil Daggett. How are you, dear?"

"Fantastic." Spencer groaned inside. Lying to Mrs. Daggett was the only way to make it through the conversation without strangling himself with the phone cord. Grandma's friends from her quilt club had no concept that a sixteen-year-old boy had no interest in quilting.

"I need some help, Spencer. Alice suggested I call you."

No! Spencer whimpered in his head, focusing to keep the dream of Duke's offer fresh in his mind.

Mrs. Daggett went on. "I was over this morning, you know, for the quilt club."

The quilt club happened so often Grandma should charge rent. And she wondered why he rarely left his room. What had she volunteered him for this time?

"I have some calico for Alice."

Spencer shifted his weight from one foot to the other. "A cat?"

A laugh that sounded like crumpling paper crackled through the receiver. "Calico fabric, dear, not a cat. Alice needs it for a project. It's very important. Can you come right away?"

Spencer hung his head in defeat. "Sure, be right over."

"Spencer? This is Lillian Daggett."

The low, rasping voice of Grandma's closest friend made me relax. Not McKaffey. Good. "Grandma's not home."

"I'm looking for you, actually. I have your lawn mowing money," Mrs. Daggett said. "Could you stop by sometime this evening? If I keep it any longer I'm afraid I might spend it on more fabric." She chuckled, but it sounded more like someone gasping for breath.

I perked up at the mention of money. I'd been saving up for a decent USB headset so I could talk to Kip while playing *Planet of Peril*. "Yeah, sure. I'll be right over." I hung up, excited about the cash. Mrs. Daggett hadn't paid me in so long she owed me, like, fifty bucks. If all went well, I'd be talking live on *PoP* tonight.

It's also wise to vary sentence length based on your characters and the current action. If you have a point of view character who rambles, he probably uses more lengthy sentences than a point of view character who doesn't talk much.

And if you have a fight scene or a battle of some kind, short sentences give the sense of excitement and fast-paced action. Long sentences do the opposite.

Make it Yours:

1. Take a look at your paragraph and sentence lengths. Can you combine short sentences or divide some long sentences to come up with a more varied flow?

2. Consider the pacing of the action in each scene and whether the scene might benefit from some shorter or longer sentences.

Making Cliché Phrases Your Own

A cliché phrase is an expression that's so common it has lost its originality. They could be idioms, which are impossible phrases like, "It's raining cats and dogs," sayings like, "there's a method to my madness," dialogue like, "Mark my words," or overused descriptions like "alabaster skin." Clichés have been used so much that they make the reader "roll her eyes."

Avoid clichés in your writing. It can be hard to find them because some are so common you don't even realize how cliché they are. But do your best to keep an eye out for them as you rewrite. If your curious, there are many websites with lists of clichés.

When you find a cliché in your story, make it your own. Tweak it a little or a lot—whatever works best for your character and storyworld. For example:

He smelled like a dirty diaper/rotten eggs.

vs.

He smelled like the outhouse after Uncle Dan used it.

We're all in the same boat.

vs.

We're all in the same wagon. (Great for a historical.)

It had coal black eyes.

vs.

It had eyes that looked like someone had blacked them out
with a Sharpie.

The voice of your character matters a great deal too.

She was higher than a kite.

vs.

She was as high as a 747. (Dad's voice.)

She was as high as the balloon my sister lost today. (Teen's voice.)

She was as high as Mariah Carey's vocal range. (Woman's voice.)

Hackneyed Plots, Twists, and Stereotypical Characters

Once upon a time (cliché phrase!) every cliché idea was new and original and so brilliant that it inspired people to copy it. But over time, so many people have used those same brilliant ideas that they're no longer brilliant, and now they make readers (or viewers) groan or roll their eyes.

Let's try to avoid having our readers groan and roll their eyes.

If something in your story is cliché, don't worry. You can still write your story, even keep the scene, though that might not be your best bet. My point? You need to be aware of what's cliché and understand that an editor, agent, or reader will likely recognize that. Then you'll want to fix the cliché to make it work in your story before you submit.

You might brainstorm ways to change the cliché. Introduce a new character. Bring back a dead character. Maybe the cliché character isn't who we thought he was. Make that cliché plot twist turn one more time with a fresh angle so that the reader thinks he knows where you're going, but you surprise him.

Readers love surprises.

Here are some other ideas to consider, but keep in mind that every character is on a journey and every scene should move your plot forward.

•Do the opposite of what you planned or do something unexpected.

•Create your own creatures or weapons and phrases. Forget dragons and elves and dwarves; swords, bows, and guns, etc. Create your own species. Create your own weapon. Have fun with it! I created chams (fire-breathing bears) and gowzals (rat-like birds) in my trilogy, and they worked pretty well.

•Vary your characters' ages. I mean, it's pretty coincidental that same-aged males and females are always going on epic journeys together, isn't it? Consider not having everyone in your story be the same age.

•Skip the prologue. Write it for yourself if you want to work out the history of your characters or storyworld, but don't put it in the book. Too many people have.

•Don't become paranoid over every little thing. No one is going to call your medieval fantasy novel cliché because your characters use swords. These are merely ideas to get you thinking. When you go back in to rewrite, work hard to make those clichés work for you. See what brilliant treasures you can come up with that are so amazing people will be copying *you*.

Cliché plots or twists to watch out for

•The love triangle.
•The line, "Don't you die on me!"
•A story about the chosen one.
•A prophecy being fulfilled.
•Prologues with an abandoned baby.
•Portals to another world.
•The sequel where the couple has split up and must be reunited.
•The magical item of great importance.
•Prologue that happens many years before your story begins.
•The best friend falls in love with the main character.
•The fake death. We saw him die, but . . . he's alive! (I did this one . . .)
•A character goes to a magic school of some kind.

•The minority sidekick OR comic relief sidekick.

•The gay best friend.

•The evil other woman, ex-wife, parent, etc. (People aren't ever THAT evil.)

•A retired guy called back into service because he's the ONLY ONE who can get the job done.

•The bad guy who is really the main character's parent.

•The minor character that's planning to retire. You know he's going to die . . . and he does!

•The "we look alike, let's switch places" plot.

•Big guys are dumb and oafish.

•Just before the big battle someone says, "Are you ready?" And your hero says, "I was born ready."

•The evil, dark lord of whatever.

•Main character is tutored by the old man. (I did this too!)

•The rakish hero who falls for the virginal heroine. He's a heart-breaker, but now he's met the one woman who can tame his wild heart. Sure.

•The bad guy could have killed the good guy but he monologues instead, giving the hero time to get away. (*cough* James Bond)

•The couple that hates each other at the beginning but end up together by the end of the book.

•The plain girl who gets a makeover and all of a sudden she's gorgeous and all the guys love her.

•The dying man's line, "Tell my wife and kids I love them!"

•The orphan who turns out to be someone really important. (And I also did this one! Oopsy.)

Make it Yours:

Do you have any clichés in your plot or subplots? How can you take that idea and tweak it so that it's new and fresh? Think about it.

*So the writer who breeds
more words than he needs,
is making a chore for
the reader who reads.*

–Dr. Seuss

13 Tightening Your Prose

by Jill

Once your book is complete, and you're combing through it in editing mode, make sure that every word counts and belongs on the page. Seek out bland words, fluff words, needless words, and poor sentence structures. Fixing these things will make your manuscript tight. It will make it sing.

Cut Needless Words

When you're writing, you may feel the urge to add lots of descriptive words to make sure the reader gets it. Adjectives are often overused and can be redundant. And fluff words, also known as modifiers, often do nothing but take up space in your manuscript. Keep in mind: less is more. Try to remember this magic formula: 1 + 1 = ½. That means, if you overuse descriptive words, you might be making the story worse, rather than better. And whenever possible, one word is better than two or more. Below are some examples of fluff and how it might be tamed a bit for tightness and clarity.

Poor: Luke was excited and thrilled.
Better: Luke was thrilled.

One emotional word at a time packs a bigger punch. Plus, "excited" and "thrilled" are redundant since they have such similar meanings. Whenever you catch two similar words together in your story, pick your favorite and delete the other.

Poor: The sculpture was totally gigantic.
Better: The sculpture was gigantic.

The word "gigantic" implies that the object is about as big as it can possibly be. The word "totally" in front of it adds nothing. Better to cut it.

Poor: Billy felt his insides freeze, and he just knew that at any moment, they would see him and beat him to a bloody pulp.

Better: Billy froze. Any second they would see him and plant him like a rose bush.

"Knew" and "felt" are telling, so they can be cut. I also got rid of the cliché, "beat him into a bloody pulp." Note: making it two sentences increased the tension. Short sentences like, "Billy froze," almost make my spine shiver.

Poor: She cared nothing of the rumbling noise in her stomach as she searched through the piles and piles of clothes, looking for her cheerleading skirt.

Better: Her stomach rumbled, but she continued digging through the mountain of laundry. Where was that skirt?

"Cared nothing" is wordy and telling. I showed her caring nothing for the rumbling noise in the second example by stating the facts: Her stomach rumbled and she continued digging.

Also, "digging" creates a more powerful word picture as to the size of the pile. "Mountain" is more specific than "piles and piles" and is two less words, and "Where was that skirt?" is stronger than "looking for her cheerleading skirt" because it shows what she's looking for and it shows her frustration.

The first sentences were twenty-five words long. My rewrite was seventeen.

Look in the Extras section for a list of weasel words, which are words you can try to cut from your manuscript.

Vague vs. Specific

As you edit, seek out vague words. They weaken your writing, confuse the reader, and it sounds like you, the author, aren't quite sure of what you're trying to say. These types of words often facilitate telling. In the following examples, I've bolded the vague words.

Sarah **was a little tired** from cheerleading practice.

John **climbed** the **tree** and **looked** at the **mountain**.

Kate ate **some** pizza and fell asleep **watching TV**.

Michael Manis is **so good looking**.

Rachel's hair **was pretty**.

What's wrong with these sentences? They're vague! They don't use words that evoke a clear picture in the reader's mind. Here are the same examples written with more specific words.

Sarah **was exhausted** from cheerleading practice.

John **shimmied** up the **swaying willow** and **gazed** at the **monstrous peak of Mt. McKinley**.

Kate ate **a whole** pizza and fell asleep **watching Doctor Who**.

Michael Manis is **Clark Kent without the geek.** He's got that **Superman build, the dark hair with the curls, the piercing blue eyes, but no glasses, stuttering, or falling all over himself.**

Rachel's hair **fell in black waves over her shoulders and down her back.**

These words are much stronger and offer a clear picture to the reader. "Sarah was exhausted from cheerleading practice" still bothers me, though, because it's telling. How about this?

Sarah entered her bedroom and tossed her duffle bag and pompoms onto the floor. She trudged across her room and fell onto the bed, muscles aching. She awoke at the sound of her mother's voice.

Whew! That's better.

As you go back through your manuscript, look for vague words that leave the reader wondering. Good writing is in the details.

Also, vague words of measurement can almost always be cut. Words like: every, often, sometimes, a little, a bit, kind of, sort of, about, nearly, etc. These words mean nothing. It's okay to use them in dialogue, but in narrative, be specific to help the reader see exactly what you mean.

Contractions

Depending on your genre, you may want to add or delete contractions from your story. If you're writing nonfiction or historical, you may not want any contractions, because the lack of contractions can make your prose sound more formal. But if you're writing contemporary or young adult, I suggest using as many contractions as you can.

Some writers prefer to only use contractions in dialogue, and that's okay too. But do keep in mind, most people use contractions when speaking. There's always a rare exception. In my book *By*

Darkness Hid, Vrell was a noblewoman, and to set her dialogue apart, I tried not to allow her to use contractions. It made her sound a little prissy, which I liked.

Tricky words

There are certain words that almost every author occasionally mistypes. It's not that the author doesn't know which word is which or can't spell, it's just, sometimes you get typing so fast and mistakes are made. And some mistakes are harder to find that others.

I like to use the Find function in Word to go back and search for some of those tricky words. It's tedious, but it makes me feel better every time I catch mistakes. And I always do. Two of my favorites to mistype are: though/through/thought and lose/loose.

Quirks and Habits

Every author forms habits that can become monotonous to the reader. I tend to add way too many metaphors and similes. I do a "Find" search for the word "like," but it's more difficult to find all my metaphors. Another habit of mine is to use triplet sentences like: He walked down the hall, got a drink from the fountain, and went outside. Triplet sentences are something I have to watch for, and my editor helps me, since he knows this is a sentence structure I overuse.

Keep an eye out for overused words or phrases that you tend to repeat.

Weasel Words

Weasel words are those pesky words that sneak into your sentences like "just" or "very." When I'm working on my final draft, I have a list of words that I do a Find search for. Again, it's tedious. But it really makes a difference in my manuscript.

Action Out of Order

Fiction should be shown in order: action, reaction. If the reader is going to connect with your characters and plot, the reader needs to experience everything the character does in a logical way, so when important actions are left out or seem to happen backwards, it disconnects the reader. For example:

> Poor: Ryan ducked to let Mike's punch go over his head.
> Better: Mike swung a punch and Ryan ducked.

> Poor: The world was foggy as I opened my eyes.
> Better: I opened my eyes to a foggy sky.

Teleporting

A mistake often made by new writers is the character that seems to teleport from one location to another. Like when someone is on the couch, then he's suddenly in the kitchen without having walked from one room to the other. For example:

> Rachel was reading her math book at her desk in Mr. Lawler's classroom when the bell rang. She opened her locker and put her book away.

But we've missed the action of her moving from the classroom to her locker, right? Fixed, it might look like this:

> Rachel was reading her math book at her desk in Mr. Lawler's classroom when the bell rang. She walked to her locker and put her book away.

Continuous action words

Trying to write things that happen simultaneously doesn't work. Watch out for words like: as, when, while, after, and continued to. I know it's tempting to use these words, especially in a fight scene, but try not to overuse them. Most of the time they can be omitted. And if you do use them, be careful to put things in logical order: action first, then reaction.

> Poor: The car stopped as Katie ran into the street.
> Better: Katie ran into the street, and the car skidded to a stop.

> Poor: Maggie cried when she dropped her pacifier.
> Better: Maggie dropped her pacifier and cried.

> Poor: Ben wrote in his journal while eating a donut.
> Better: Ben wrote in his journal and munched on a donut.

Infinite Verb Phrases (Starting sentences with —ing words)

Avoid starting a sentence with a word that ends in "ing" because such words imply everything in the sentence is happening simultaneously, creating physical impossibilities.

> Poor: Grabbing a notebook, he stuffed it in his backpack, slammed his locker, and ran to class.

> Better: He grabbed a notebook, stuffed it in his backpack, slammed the locker, and ran to class.

Since he can't physically grab a notebook, stuff it into his backpack, slam the locker door, and run to class simultaneously, the first example isn't humanly possible.

Progressive Tense

Progressive tense uses an active verb with an -ing ending and a helping verb. Most of the time, it's shorter and more accurate to use the simple past tense of the verb. If you want to convey that something is in the process of happening, use progressive tense. Otherwise, edit it out.

Past Progressive tense: Jane was walking to practice.
Past tense: Jane walked to practice.

Double Verbs

Watch out for sentences using "started to" and "began to." These double verbs imply that an interruption happened. The character began or started an action, but something stopped him. Now if you are implying that something did interrupt the action, using these words is appropriate. Take a look at the following examples:

Kaylee began to tug on the handle of her purse. —This means she began to tug on her purse handle but never quite managed to do it.

Kaylee tugged on the handle of her purse. —Here she actually succeeded and tugged on the handle.

Mike started to clean his room. —This implies that he's not going to finish.

Mike started to clean his room, but his cell phone rang. —This is better because it gives the reader the interruption to match the use of "started to."

Mike cleaned his room. —This tells us that he did the entire job.

Make it Yours:
Read the Self-Editing Checklists and the list of weasel words in the Extras section of this book, then go through your manuscript and see what you can cut out.

Passive vs. Active Writing
by Stephanie

Passive writing is an issue for a lot of new writers, and often they don't even realize it. I had no idea I had an issue with it until a literary agent told me she liked my story, but that my sentence structure was way too passive. "If you can fix that, I'll take another look," she said.

"Sure!" I told her. "I'll revise and get it right back to you!"

And then I set about trying to figure out what in the heck she was talking about. *Passive writing?!?!*

I sat at my desk with *Garner's Modern American Usage*, *The Elements of Style*, and *The Chicago Manual of Style*. In each one, I looked up what they had to say about using an "active voice." And then I reread the article. And then I reread again. Then I studied my manuscript. Then I turned back to the books and read the articles out loud.

After doing all that, I thought I maybe-kinda-sorta knew what the style guides were talking about and thought I could possibly fix it.

The first thing I had to figure out was what it meant to write in a passive voice. The word "was" is a good clue that you're speaking in a passive voice, or "is" if you're writing is present tense. These are some examples ripped straight out of an old manuscript of mine. I've bolded the passive phrases:

It was finally Kyle who led her out of there.
Carter was there before she could do or say anything.
It was Carter's best friend Matt who asked the question.

115

These can easily be revised to an active voice:

Kyle led her out of there.
Carter arrived before she could do or say anything.
Matt, Carter's best friend, asked the question.

To quote the wisdom of William Strunk Jr., author of *The Elements of Style*, "The active voice is usually more direct and vigorous than the passive." Which I think is displayed in the sentences above. The ones written in an active voice are just better sentences.

But was (or "is") is not an evil word. It can be used to describe something ongoing. Like:

When I entered, Jane was stirring the soup.

James was a handsome boy.

The room was decorated in mauve and blue.

I was scrubbing the floors when Lara called.

All fine uses. Because if you changed that first one to something like, "When I entered, Jane stirred the soup," it would take on a different meaning. It would sound like Jane saw you enter, and then she stirred the soup.

Make it Yours:
   Search your manuscript for the word "was" (or "is" if you're writing in the present tense). Consider your usage of it—is it necessary, or could you write your sentence in a more active way?

It's not wise to violate rules until you know how to observe them.
—T. S. Eliot

14 Formatting It Right

Technicalities
by Jill

Formatting your manuscript correctly for the first time can be seriously intimidating. Here are some quick bullet points to get you started:

• Your title page should be single spaced. The rest of the manuscript should be double spaced.

• Use 12-point Times New Roman or Courier font. No exceptions. Don't use a fancy font—it'll mark you as an amateur.

• Each chapter should begin on a new page. Don't hit "Enter, Enter, Enter" to get your cursor to a new page. You must insert a Page Break at the end of each chapter, then begin typing a new one.

• Start each chapter ¼ to ⅓ of the way down the page.

• Double space your manuscript.

• Use only one space after punctuation, not two.

• Avoid all fancy formatting, like drop cap letters to the start of each chapter, flowery scene breaks, or any other decorative graphics.

• Don't put a copyright symbol on your manuscript (See the Q&A section for the reason why).

On the next few pages you'll find examples for what the first few pages of your manuscript should look like. I've created video tutorials to walk you through how to format everything using Microsoft Word. To find them, visit:

www.jillwilliamson.com/teenage-authors/writing-podcast-tutorials/

1" margins on all four sides

Use 12-point, Times New Roman or Courier font on all manuscripts.

Center chapter title 1/4 to 1/2 of the way down the page. Make sure that all other chapters start in the same place.

Set indentations to .05 and double-space your text.

Chapter One

Martyr stared at the equation on the whiteboard and set his pencil down. He didn't feel like practicing math today. What did math matter when his expiration date was so near?

His wrist still throbbed from Fido's teeth. Martyr touched the strip of fabric he'd ripped from his bedsheet and tied around his wrist to stop the bleeding. He hoped the wound would heal before a doctor noticed it. A trip upstairs to mend it would be unpleasant, as the doctor would likely use the opportunity to perform tests. Martyr shuddered.

To distract himself, he glanced at the other boys. Every Jason in the classroom except Speedy and Hummer scribbled down the numbers from the whiteboard. Speedy sketched Dr. Max's profile, staring at the doctor with intense concentration. His hand

1

```
┌─────────────────────────────────────────────────────────────┐
│                                      Type your title / last name / │
│  ┌─────────────────────────┐         page number in the header. │
│  │ 1" margins on all four sides │     The page number doesn't      │
│  └─────────────────────────┘         have to go in the header.   │
│     REPLICATION / Williamson / 2      You can center it on the    │
│                                       bottom of each page or      │
│                                       tab it over to the far right.│
│     darted over the paper, shading the dark face with a short, black beard.│
│                                                                │
│        Hummer—as always—hummed and rocked back and forth, hugging himself.│
│                                                                │
│     Martyr never understood why the doctors made Hummer take classes instead of putting│
│                                                                │
│     him in with the brokens. Perhaps it had to do with Hummer's being so much older than│
└─────────────────────────────────────────────────────────────┘
```

"Correctly" Using Italics
by Stephanie

There are no hard rules about "Don't italicize your character's thoughts" but it's rather frowned upon. Kind of like overusing exclamation points or adverbs, too many italicized thoughts can give your manuscript an amateur aura, which of course you want to avoid.

You especially want to avoid italicized thoughts in a book written in first person (I walked, I sat) since you're already so clearly in the character's head. Here's an example:

I walked through the door into eerie silence. *Why is it so quiet in here?* "Mom?"

Revising it with no italics makes it so much smoother and—I think—deeper:

I walked through the door into eerie silence. Why was it so quiet? "Mom?"

For those writing in third person, I better understand the writer's temptation to italicize:

John walked through the door into eerie silence. *Why is it so quiet in here?* "Mom?"

The writer wants us to know what John is thinking, wants to dip into John's head so we can see the thought scrolling through his mind. We, the reader, want that too . . . but are the italics necessary? Consider this:

John walked through the door into eerie silence. Why was it so quiet? "Mom?"

You still get that it's a thought, don't you? Again, it's because the writer has already established who we're following—John. Therefore we understand, without help from the font, that John is the one wondering why it's so quiet.

But what if you write your stories in an omniscient POV? I won't pretend to be an expert on using omniscient POV, but I still think you should avoid italicized thoughts. Because even with an omniscient narrator where we, the reader, might pop into the several different minds in one scene, the writer still needs to have established which character we're talking about in that moment.

Like Cecily von Ziegesar does here in *You Know You Love Me* (a Gossip Girl book):

Blair nodded impatiently. What did Ms. Glos think she was, a moron?

Even though that book is written with an omniscient narrator, the writer signals, "Hey, it's Blair's turn on the stage" by starting the sentence with her name.

So when *should* you italicize sentences?

Sometimes dream sequences work better in italics. Especially if it's a book that has several short ones throughout. (*Out with the In Crowd* does and my editor suggested putting the dreams in italics. It worked well for that situation.)

Prayers, especially "breath prayers" like *Thank you, Lord* or *Little help here, God?*

Also, you might run across the occasional thought that just plain works better in italics. I've had that in a few manuscripts and the only common thread I can pick out is that they're extremely vulnerable, involuntary character thoughts. I actually spotted one in *You Know You Love Me,* again by Cecily Von Ziegesar.

Dan nodded. *Do you have to go?* He was afraid to open his mouth . . .

That works and falls into that category I mentioned above. He desperately wants Serena to stay there with him, and that's his gut reaction when she says she's heading home.

So don't automatically unitalicize every thought in your manuscript, just determine why you chose to format it that way.

Punctuation
by Jill

Punctuation had never been my favorite thing. But I needed to learn the rules to be a professional author. And so do you.

Trust me.

One mistake here or there won't get you rejected. But if your manuscript is filled with punctuation errors and misspellings, an agent or editor won't keep reading.

They will reject you.

We don't want to turn this book into an English punctuation textbook, so we've decided to include the top punctuation errors we see again and again in manuscripts.

I highly recommend picking up a punctuation book for your own reference. *The Chicago Manual of Style* is the reference for the book publishing industry. Add a used copy to your wish list. It's a great tool to have on your shelf.

Punctuating Dialogue

Stephanie talks about this in Chapter 9, but I'll briefly cover the rules here as well.

Said Tags

A said tag assigns the dialogue to a speaker by using the word "said" or a variation of that word (asked, yelled, whispered, etc). A said tag is connected to the dialogue with a comma, unless the dialogue is a question or requires an exclamation point. When using a said tag, the pronoun must be lowercase unless you are using a proper name. Pay attention to the underlined parts of the examples below for proper punctuation.

"I'm sorry," the girl said.

"I am the President of the United States," Abraham said.

"What do you want?" she asked.

"What do you want?" Kate asked.

"Leave me alone!" he screamed.

"Leave me alone!" Mike screamed.

"I can't believe I'm telling you this," Mindy said, "but I'm one of them." (Since the said tag interrupted the dialogue, a comma was used on both sides of the said tag. If you do this, make sure the interruption falls in a natural place for your character to pause. Read the dialogue out loud to see what sounds best.)

"I can't believe I'm telling you this," Mindy said. "I'm one of them." (Here the said tag came between two complete sentences.)

Mindy took a deep breath and said, "I can't believe I'm telling you this, but I'm one of them." (The "Mindy took a deep breath" part of the example is what's called an action tag. But if you combine action with a said tag, like I did in this example, you need to punctuate the sentence like you would for a said tag.)

A Note from Jill about Exclamation Points

Editors and agents like to say that an author is allowed only one exclamation point per manuscript. It's a joke, but there's a grain of truth to it. Their point? Use exclamation points rarely. They're distracting to readers and should only be used when your character is screaming. Let your dialogue show other forms of anger or attitude. And save the exclamation points for special occasions.

Action Tags

An action tag is a complete sentence that identifies the speaker by what he's doing. Because we see a character's action in the same paragraph as dialogue, we know he's the speaker. Since action tags are sentences, they're punctuated like sentences.

Krista rolled her eyes and sighed. "What do you want, Paul?"

"Get out!" Beth slammed the door in her mother's face.

"If you want to come, get in." Kyle opened the car door. "Just don't be mad at me if you get in trouble for missing curfew."

"If you want to come, get in," Kyle opened the car door, "but don't be mad at me if you get in trouble for missing curfew." (This example used an action tag to interrupt the sentence.)

In special cases when an action interrupts dialogue in a quick way, you can use em dashes to set this off. Since the break belongs to the sentence, rather than the dialogue inside, the em dashes must appear outside the quotation marks.

124

"Before we start"—the knight plunged one of the blades into the grassy soil—"we need to go over the basics."

Commas with Coordinating Conjunctions

There are seven coordinating conjunctions: and, but, for, nor, or, so, and yet. Basically, these are words that connect two clauses in a sentence. If you have a sentence that has one of those seven words in the middle, how do you know when you need a comma before the conjunction or not?

Simple. If the words on both sides of the conjunction are complete sentences by themselves, you need the comma to avoid having a run-on sentence.

"Almost everyone on earth likes chocolate, but I can't stand how sweet it tastes."

You need the comma before "but" because "Almost everyone on earth likes chocolate" is a complete sentence and so is "I can't stand how sweet it tastes."

If the sentence had one side that wasn't a complete sentence on its own, a comma would be incorrect. "Almost everyone on earth likes chocolate but not carrots." Since "not carrots" is not a complete sentence, a comma is not needed.

NOTE: For a very short sentence, you can omit the comma.

The bus departed and we were on our way.

Commas After an Introductory Word Group

When you start a sentence with an introductory word group, you need to separate it from the rest of the sentence with a comma. A good rule of thumb is if the introductory word group is five words or more, use a comma. Less than five words, it's optional.

When Martin was ready to eat, the waiter brought him a salad to start with.

NOTE: The comma can be omitted here in a very short sentence.

In no time we were in a different state.

Commas Between Items in a Series

When three or more items are listed in a series, those items should be separated with commas. This applies to single words, phrases, or clauses. Note that a comma goes before the conjunction at the end of the sentence.

My favorite candy is M&M's, Skittles, and Gummi Bears.

You can choose from going on a hike up the mountain, playing paintball in the field, going on a canoe ride, or swimming in the pool.

Commas Between Coordinating Adjectives vs.
No Commas Between Cumulative Adjectives

Adjectives are coordinate if they can be joined with "and" or if they can be scrambled and still make sense. Commas are required between coordinate adjectives.

Michael is a strong, tall, talented basketball player.

To test this example we first see if we can join the adjectives with "and" and keep the same meaning.

Michael is a strong and tall and talented basketball player.

Next we scramble the adjectives to see if this has an effect.

Michael is a talented, strong, tall basketball player.

Same meaning? Yep!

Cumulative adjectives lean on one another, with each modifying a larger word group. They do not require commas in between. How do you know that they're cumulative, though?

Four gleaming white doves flew toward me.

"Gleaming" modifies "white." "Four" modifies "gleaming white." And when we test this sample joining the adjectives with "and" it doesn't work.

Four and gleaming and white and doves flew toward me.

When we scramble them, it also changes the meaning.

Gleaming four white doves flew toward me.

This doesn't work nor does, "White gleaming four doves flew toward me."

The Colon

A colon means *as follows*. It's used to introduce something (or a series of things).

1. Use a colon after a complete sentence to direct attention to a list.

Marcia's daily workout was supposed to include at least the following: twenty sit-ups, ten push-ups, and fifteen minutes of cardio.

Give us the following construction materials: wood, hammers, and nails.

This summer our family plans to visit four western states: Arizona, Utah, Colorado, and New Mexico.

2. Use a colon after a complete sentence to direct attention to an appositive: A word or phrase that means the same thing.

Shelby was shocked at what she saw: her reflection.

We found the cat sleeping in her favorite spot: the tree in the backyard.

There's one obstacle I must conquer before graduation: passing all my classes.

3. Use a colon after a complete sentence to direct attention to a quotation.

Consider the words of Mother Theresa: "Even the rich are hungry for love, for being cared for, for being wanted, for having someone to call their own."

Capitalization and the Colon

How do you know whether or not to capitalize the first word following a colon? Always have the word be lowercase except in the following circumstances:

1. If the first word is a proper noun.

The people who should be on the bus are the following: Mark, Christa, Drew, and Kelley.

2. If the colon precedes a definition or a direct quote.

When Christy got angry at Karen, Jill told her not to "Jake Out": An act of turning into a werewolf, inspired by the book *Twilight*.

The poignant words of Douglas Adams state: "Flying is learning how to throw yourself at the ground and miss."

3. If the colon comes before two or more related sentences.

Robert had three options: He could walk the six miles to the library. He could call someone and beg a ride. Or he could just take Grandma Nan's car.

4. If the colon introduces dialogue lines in a speech or drama.

Juliette: Then, window, let day in, and let life out.
Romeo: Farewell, farewell! One kiss and I'll descend.

The Semicolon

1. A semicolon is used to separate closely related independent clauses not joined by a coordinating conjunction.
Say what?
Basically, use a semicolon if you want to glue two sentences together that are similar.

"Hate begets hate; violence begets violence; toughness begets a greater toughness." —Martin Luther King, Jr.

Ten finalists performed to be the next American Idol; only two remain.

Mr. Sanchez is a great chef; however, he won't eat his own cooking.

Each of the independent clauses (sets of words between the semicolons) are complete sentences on their own. You can't use a semicolon if these are only phrases. You also can't use a semi colon if you have a coordinating conjunction (and, but, or) between the sentences.

If you did put a comma where a semicolon is above, you will have created a comma splice, which is a very icky grammar error. Be sure to look carefully at all your clauses. If they are complete sentences, you need a semicolon. If they aren't, you don't need a semicolon.

2. A semicolon is also used between items in a series that contain internal punctuation.

Some popular fantasy novels are *Harry Potter and the Sorcerer's Stone*, with the boy wizard with a lightning bolt scar; *Eragon*, about a young dragon rider; and the timeless *The Lion, the Witch, and the Wardrobe*, where four siblings enter a magical land through a wardrobe.

Dashes

There are two kinds of dashes that are used most often in fiction writing: the em dash—and the en dash–

Please note that there should be NO SPACE before or after either type of dash.

The Em Dash

To create the em dash, type a word, then type two hyphens, then type the next word, then type a space. Do not put any spaces until you are done with the sequence.

What you type will look like this: word--word(space)

When you hit that last space bar, the two dashes will convert to an em dash.

NOTE: If you read Harry Potter, you'll see spaces with her dashes. Keep in mind that J. K. Rowling is a British author and the punctuation and grammar rules are different there. These are the rules for the United States.

1. Use an em dash to set off parenthetical material that you want to emphasize.

Everything that went wrong—from her C- on our history project to Tom breaking up with her—Shelly blamed on me.

Can you believe that Megan Walker—a band geek and a freshman—won homecoming queen?

2. Use an em dash to set off appositives that contain commas.

When you apply the make-up—foundation, mascara, eye shadow, and lipstick—be sure to follow the guidelines.

3. Use an em dash to signify a break in thought.

"I have so much to—did you just say she had the baby?"

4. Use an em dash to signify an interruption.

"I don't know why it happened. Maybe it's because—"

The En Dash

To create the en dash, type a word, type a space, then type one hyphen, then type the next word, then type a space. What you type will look like this: word(space)-word(space)

When you hit that last space bar, the dash will convert to an en dash. NOTE: Once the dash is converted, go back and take out the first space. There should be no spaces before or after a dash.

1. Use an en dash to connect inclusive numbers such as: page numbers, dates, or Bible references. Here the en dash means "up to and including" or "through."

Please read in your text pages 86—92.

I went to college from 1993—1997.

I read John 3:16—17 and it changed my life.

Ellipses

Ellipses are used to show thought trailing off. If your character is confused, insecure, uncertain, falling asleep, or passing out, an ellipsis is the tool you want to use to convey this. Put a space before and after an ellipsis, unless it's beside another punctuation.

"Where could it . . . I had it right . . . the medallion, I . . . I must have dropped it!"

"I want to go there . . . first thing . . . in the morning."

". . . tell you who shot me. It was . . ." Kit's body went limp in John's arms.

Apostrophes

Use an apostrophe to replace omitted letters in a word. If your font uses curly quotes, make sure that the apostrophe curls in the right direction. Whether the missing letter is in the front, middle, or end of a word, it should always curl to the left, like this: '

Take note that omitting letters can be distracting to the reader, so don't overdo it.

"There be no tellin' what he'll do now." (The apostrophe takes the place of the "g" in "telling.")

"All you kids do is sit around listening to that loud rock 'n' roll." (The apostrophe before the "n" takes the place of the "a" in "and." The apostrophe after the "n" takes the place of the "d" in "and.")

"Daddy, tell me the story 'bout the princess and the toad." (The apostrophe takes the place of the "a" in "about.")

Numbers

Numbers can be written two ways: spelled out in letters (two) or written in numerals (2). The rules are: Spell out numbers one through one hundred. Spell out rounded numbers (hundreds, millions). Spell out numbers in reference to age. Spell out all numbers that begin a sentence. Use numerals (1234) for all other numbers.

Michael crouched down. "There are millions of ants here!"

"I need fifty copies of the flyer," Megan said.

"I need 2,500 copies of the flyer," Megan said.

"She's ninety-six years old!"

"One, I can't understand why you hate me. And, two, I don't like you either."

Time

Always spell out the time of day unless you're referring to the exact time.

Drew went to bed at five o'clock exhausted from the tournament.

"Mom slept in and I missed my nine-thirty dentist appointment."

"I get to church way early because the Sunday bus goes by my house at 7:10."

"Class starts directly at 8:35 tomorrow morning. Don't be late!"

Dates

Dates are written with numerals. Do not write August 1st. The correct methods are:

> August 1.
>
> "On January 1, 2000, there were no major fallouts due to the new millennium."
>
> "The photograph is copyright April 1942."
>
> On 5 February, 1903 Mario and his family arrived in America.

When a day is mentioned without the month or year, spell out the number.

> "By the fifteenth, finals will be over and we can focus on the Christmas holidays!"

Whatever it takes to finish things, finish. You will learn more from a glorious failure than you ever will from something you never finished.

—Neil Gaiman

15 How to Know When You're Done

by Stephanie

This is a question we hear a lot, and it's so hard to know how to answer. Because when it's early in your writing journey and it seems you learn more about writing and storytelling every day, it can feel impossible to discern when to stop fussing with your manuscript. So how do you know when it's time to take the plunge and share your book with your critique partner or start querying literary agents?

I'm going to start with a question that totally marks me as a mom: Have you done your best?

Your book isn't perfect, of course, but did you do your best with the knowledge and skills you have? Or were you lazy with character development? Is that plot twist at the end more of a cheap trick? Did you have an idea for how to improve it . . . but you weren't in the mood for yet another rewrite?

If you've written and rewritten and revised and edited and rewritten and revised again, and you feel this is the best story you can produce at this point in your journey, I say go for it. Send out the queries. See what happens. I honestly didn't know if my writing was "there" or not, until an agent said, "I'm so excited about this project. Can you send me the rest right now?"

And I didn't dare say it out loud, but when she said that, my internal monologue was, "Really? I did it? It's good enough now?"

I had been pitching projects for a few years at that point, but I never really knew if they were ready or not. I did my best with the knowledge and skill I had, put it out there, and braced myself for the feedback.

This is a rather uncomfortable way to determine the quality of your writing abilities, but it's about the truest mirror you'll find. Not to say that agents and editors don't make judgments in error or guess wrongly about what will sell and what the public wants. Most everyone has received at least a handful of rejections. But for my rejections, typically I knew in my gut if they were right or not.

Like on the first book I sent out. Hardly any editors bothered to read it (no surprise, since I printed out all 90 pages of it and mailed it to anyone who accepted unsolicited manuscripts), but the one who did told me my ending lacked oomph. And you know, that resonated. As I considered it, I realized my book didn't have an ending at all.

By now, I have a definite procedure I follow before I declare myself done with a book.

Before I send anything to my agent or editor, I always:

1. Write a bare bones first draft
2. Let my draft sit for six weeks (unless we're on a major time crunch, but ideally I take a full six weeks).
3. Do the macro edit.
4. Do the micro edit.
5. Send to my critique partner and wait for her thoughts.
6. Make her suggested changes and read through it again for typos.
7. Send it to my agent.

And to be honest, even as a published author, when weeks go by and I haven't heard back from my agent, I slide into a pit of thoughts like, "She hates it. She's wondering why she ever took me on as a client." Every time the phone rings, I'm thinking, "It's her. She's calling to say she hates it." Most my writer friends do something similar. We're a needy bunch.

While I've gained confidence in my ability to know if my story is a good idea or not, and while I'm mostly confident in my writing style and voice, I still tremble a bit before I send my stuff out, for whatever's that's worth to you. But at some point, you've got to go for it.

Make Your Good Book GREAT
Editing Issues That Don't Happen On the Page

A note from Jill

Writing is a solitary and emotional business. And working in isolation tends to create self-doubt, especially in an industry like publishing.

I started writing in 2004. It was August 2006 before I sold my first article. And, no, that one article didn't pay enough to support my family. I wrote some more articles, but since I wanted to be a fiction writer, I spent most my time writing books. My first book got published in 2009. And it was published with a small publisher that didn't pay advances. So it was another year before I saw any money for my efforts.

That's a long time to work without seeing any results.

Now, I wasn't writing books to make money. I wanted to get published, sure, but it was fun and I wanted to put stories out there for teen readers that were entertaining and inspiring.

That's still my goal today. But I struggle with wondering if I'm making a difference, if anyone is reading my books, whether or not I have anything of value to say. I get hurt when reviewers are cruel or don't even try to see my heart in a story. I struggle with procrastination when I have deadlines. And I am always trying to find a balance between work and family.

It's a lonely business. I'm on my own, typing stories, trying to decide if they're interesting or not, always on the lookout for new test readers to give me honest feedback. And there were people who never thought I'd succeed, people who thought I was crazy, people in my church who don't know I write books . . . and people who think I'm famous. (I'm so not!) It's a strange job, writing. You have to really love it to put up with all this weird stuff.

Good thing I love it, huh?

Don't let anyone look down on you because you are young.
—1 Timothy 4:12

16 Self-Doubt & Others' Expectations

by Stephanie

Once upon a time, I knew my writing was hot stuff.

It was well-known among my friends that I wanted to be a writer. Anytime I wrote so much as a chapter, I immediately passed it out to a few friends and asked for their feedback . . . but what I really meant was, "Tell me how wonderful this is, please."

I craved their approval.

And when they thought it was amazing, my day was awesome.

When they suggested a character seemed flat or a plot line seemed implausible, I argued. Sometimes out loud, but mostly in my head. They didn't understand it, did they? They didn't get it! What do they know, anyhow?!

This is a horrible rollercoaster ride to be on. And I wasn't smart enough to take myself off.

Instead, I got bucked off the ride. When my best friend told me my stories were boring and unimaginative, that I was wasting my time and she couldn't imagine me ever getting published, something inside me broke. On the outside I was snarky and vicious, but on the inside I was curled up in the fetal position, broken and—I thought—permanently scarred.

It took me years to come back from that, to recover both from the blow from my friend and also my dependence on the opinions of others. Here's what helped me to break free (somewhat) of my need for others' approval:

I wrote my first draft behind closed doors.

This isn't for everybody, but this made a huge difference for me, and I encourage you to give it a try at least once. Nobody sees my first drafts. Ever. I don't even like sitting next to my loving, supportive husband on the couch when I'm working on a first draft.

Until I've done my macro and micro edits, I don't let anyone read the book. Otherwise I get too many voices going on in my head and I lose track of getting the story on the page. I start focusing on the wrong things—if it's good feedback, I get preoccupied with how amazing my story is. If it's bad feedback, I get preoccupied with how much it sucks.

There's certainly a time when feedback and collaboration is fruitful and necessary . . . but for me it's *not* during the first draft. That time is for me and my characters only.

One plus I hadn't expected when I first started closing my door was how it honed my voice as an author. I wasn't thinking things like, "Oh, Christine is going to gush when she reads this scene!" Or, "I should put in a steamy kiss because Lauren likes those." Instead my focus was on telling the story as it came to me, not on pleasing my friends.

Expectations and Trust

My first readers are people who I know love me, who have my best interests at heart, and who I know like my stories and writing. In short, I trust they will speak truth to me out of love, and I trust that they won't try to take over my story and make it theirs, but that they'll instead try to strengthen it in a way that fits with my voice and my genre.

Something that helped me open up to others again was clarifying my expectations. I would say something like, "I'm interested in how such-and-such plot thread feels to you, and if you have any ideas for making this character more unique." Not only does this help me get the feedback that I really want, it's helpful to me to release the notion that I think this is perfect. Somehow telling them, "I know this isn't perfect, I just don't know how to improve it," softens the blow for me when I get the critique back.

I also do this whenever I'm critiquing for someone. Does she want general guidance? A line edit? Are there story threads I should be paying careful attention to? This saves everyone time.

Baby steps, baby rejections

Eventually, if you want to get published, you have to start submitting your stuff to agents and editors. This can be incredibly scary. I found it best to query a few agents at a time so that if I received feedback I wanted to incorporate, I would have a stronger piece to show other agents.

Sometimes you get sharp, well-defined criticism—I don't like your main character, your plot feels cliché.

Sometimes it's too vague to know what to do with it—this doesn't work for me.

And sometimes it's just a form letter.

Every editor and agent has different preferences, and just because one of them thinks your plot is boring doesn't mean they all will. If it's something you *keep* hearing, you'll want to weigh it differently than if it's something you only heard once.

Dealing with others' lack of understanding

The process of getting published is mysterious to the average person, which means many people won't understand what you're doing. And, honestly, you just have to figure out a way to be okay with that.

People will think the process should be moving along faster—you should have been done with that book months ago, or if you were really good you would have an agent by now, and what's your backup plan for when this writing thing doesn't pan out?

You'll get bad advice from people who may truly want to help you but have no knowledge of the industry. Some of the advice I received along the way was:

1. Just go to Kinkos, get your book printed and bound, and sell it like that.

2. Print out that great bit of dialogue you wrote and send it to several agents saying, "This is what I'm capable of. Can you help me get published?"

3. Write wizard stuff. That seems to be selling.

4. Get an English degree so you can get a job at a publishing house. You can make connections and work your way "up" to writing a novel.

This is just part of the writing life, people not understanding the industry or your genre or how you make money. You can let it make you crazy, or you can smile, nod, say thank you for their interest in your career, and move on with your day.

And that's one of the reasons I urge you to find a community of writers to support and be supported by. I'm fortunate that my family is incredibly supportive of my writing, but nobody understands the sting of a rejection or the frustration of a lousy writing day or the triumph of typing THE END quite like my writer friends.

You may delay,
but time will not.
—Benjamin Franklin

17 Wrestling with Procrastination

by Jill

Before I was published, procrastination wasn't such a big deal. I really didn't have any deadlines. And even when I set my own deadlines, they were for me alone, to try and achieve certain word counts.

Those are good deadlines.

But once I was published, deadlines became a lot more solid and necessary. My editors set the deadlines, and I didn't dare miss one.

My first deadline wasn't much of a big deal. I had written and edited *By Darkness Hid* until I thought it was perfect before I sold it to Marcher Lord Press. Once I signed the contract, I turned in the manuscript and waited for my edits. I started tinkering around with book two, but I figured I had time.

Then came a content edit. My editor had made a list of problems he saw with the story and asked me to rewrite those things. I was pretty excited about his edits. They were things that made me say, "Duh, Jill. How could you have missed that?"

So I completed the edits and sent them back. A short while later I received the line edit. This was a much more severe edit, and my editor wanted it back ASAP! That surprised me. I really thought I had written a clean book. But I was about to find out that most editors have a lot of feedback to give.

Panic set in, and I worked hard to get the edits done. There were a few more stages this time around. Little things. But I had done it! I was a published author.

Then my editor asked me how soon I could have book two ready.

Uh . . . book two?

That was the beginning of a very stressful year. Up until that point, I wrote whatever book I wanted to write. I had no rules or deadlines. I did what I wanted. But now I had a deadline for a book that I hadn't written yet. And worse, I had readers to please. I had been getting great feedback on *By Darkness Hid*, and I didn't want to disappoint my readers!

It was a rough time of forcing myself to write, even when I didn't want to. And book three was no different. Once I finished the trilogy, I had the privilege of selling a book from a proposal. I thought that was pretty cool, until I got my deadline.

Yikes! Here we go again.

And that's the reality of being a writer. Deadlines come. Publishers are looking for authors who can work fast and deliver. I'm still not sure how successful I am in that regard. But I'm learning. And I work hard. And the deadlines keep coming.

Even though it may not always feel like it, it's truly a blessing to have deadlines.

How to deal with Procrastination

Procrastination comes in a lot of forms and usually stems from not being prepared, fear of failure, or simple boredom with the project. No matter the reason, it all gets the same result: nothing is done and you are frustrated. Here are some things I've learned to do to beat procrastination.

Set Goals

You may or may not already have a deadline. If not, set one for yourself. Then do some math to figure out how many words you need to write each day to reach your deadline. It gives you a concrete goal to strive for each time you sit down to write.

Get Organized

This is why I like plotting my story out in advance. Because it gives me a To Do list of scenes to follow so that I have a basic idea of what I should be writing each day. I also keep my notes and any reference books I'm using beside the computer so that I have everything I'll need at hand.

Skip Ahead

When I'm really stuck, or I've come up on a difficult scene that needs some serious brainstorming time, I often skip ahead to a scene that will be easier to write. This way I don't waste my computer time, and I get my word count in. I can brainstorm later in the car or when I'm cleaning the house to figure my way out of that difficult scene.

Give Up Perfectionism

Your first draft doesn't have to be good. You can come in and fix it later. And if you're working on a deadline, sometimes you have to force yourself to get that story done. Some writers get dreamy about their jobs and wait too long for inspiration to strike. But when you're on a deadline, you can't afford to wait. Make yourself do the hard work. There will be time to edit later on.

Get Rid of Distractions

It's far too easy to get distracted when you work from home. I have a rule that I try to check my email in fifteen minutes at the start of each workday. Then I close it. Facebook too. If I don't, I'll "reward myself" with little visits throughout the day, and those visits are BIG trouble.

When I write, I also tend to make excuses to get up from the computer that involve an endless sampling of snacks and beverages. So it's best for me to get a few snacks and fill my water bottle before I start my day. And if I don't have something, I can live until lunch.

Interruptions come too. If I worked at an office across town, people wouldn't stop by or call me at work. But since I work from home, people tend to think, "Jill's home," then call or stop by. And five to ten minutes here and there adds up when I'm on a deadline.

So, if I'm working toward my daily word count and the phone or doorbell rings, I usually don't answer. This might sound cruel, but if it's that important, the person will leave a message or call back. If it's later in the day and I'm working on something less important, I might answer. And I'll certainly answer if I'm expecting someone. But I can't allow myself to get interrupted otherwise.

I know writers who like to go sit at Starbucks or the library to get away from the distractions of home. If this helps you, do it. Whatever it takes to get the job done.

Make it Yours:

1. Keep a log of how much time you spend doing certain activities. How much time do you spend on email? Facebook? Snacking? Talking on the phone or texting? Writing?

2. Evaluate and try to set a more productive schedule for yourself.

Step 2

Learning the Ropes of the Publishing Industry

A note from Stephanie

I believe at the core of my being that if I can get published, *anyone* can.

When I started on my journey of becoming a novelist, all I had was a love for writing stories.

I lived in Kansas City—a great town, but hardly a publishing mecca.

I didn't know anybody even remotely connected to the industry, not even a bookstore employee.

And I didn't have a clue about what I was doing. I didn't know what genre I wrote, or that my characters should have goals, or what literary agents did, or what a query letter was.

Everything I learned, I learned by doing it wrong first. In this chapter, we hope to equip you with some etiquette and procedural basics to make your path to publication smoother than mine.

A note from Jill

There's a lot of advice out there for writers. And you can't follow it all. Believe me, I tried. But this is a wonderful industry, and there are so many great opportunities out there for you to connect.

When I first started writing, I sought out information from all kinds of sources. I gave and gave, and sometimes no one gave back. I learned the hard way what worked or what didn't work. But I got involved, I tried my best, and over time I made many friendships. (*An aside from Stephanie: This is so true. When I'm with Jill at a conference, there are constantly people stopping to say hi to her.*)

Always keep in mind, you can't please everyone. You can't become critique partners with every writer. You'll find some reviewers out there who don't read your book. *Publisher's Weekly* might hate your book. Try. Learn. Have fun. And always try to make wise choices based on what you've learned.

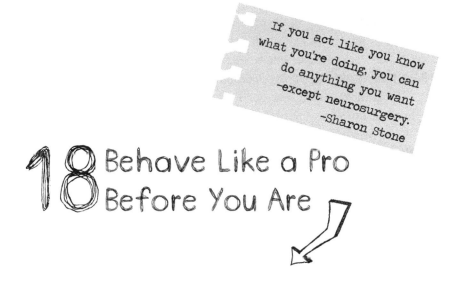

If you act like you know what you're doing, you can do anything you want —except neurosurgery.
   –Sharon Stone

18 Behave Like a Pro Before You Are

by Stephanie

Shakespeare once said, "All the world's a stage." And that's never been truer than it is now with all the ways to put yourself out there with social media and blogs and review sites. So when you're dipping your toe into the industry pool, put into practice these five guidelines of professionalism:

Guideline #1
Whatever you put out there, assume agents and editors will see it.

When an agent or editor comes across a writer they're interested in, one of the first things many of them do is run a Google search on the author. Which is why I assume that anything I say online will be seen by my agent or editor.

In reality, they're busy people and may not see very much of it. (Though I've had my agent say things to me like, "I assume you're still at the wedding," when I never told her, she just saw pictures of me at a wedding on Facebook.) But it's so much safer to run everything through the filter of, "My agent/editor will see this."

Unlike real life where we can't edit words after they've emerged from our mouths (a sad truth for those of us who aren't particularly articulate), we can edit our written words to our heart's content. We have total control over what's on our social media sites.

This means when you get a rejection, it's a bad idea to blast the agency or house on your blog. Or if you write humor, you don't want all your tweets to be depressing. If you write romance, refrain from spending all your time talking about how boys are stupid and marriage is nothing more than a piece of paper.

You don't have to be someone you're not—in fact, I'd recommend against it—just keep in mind it's not just your friends who'll see it.

Guideline #2

Use your name

If you're beginning the process of querying agents or joining writers organizations, now is a good time to shed any email addresses or Twitter handles that involve things like, OneDirectionRawks@email.com or yurboyfrndwantsme@email.com.

Now is the time to get your own adult email address, which should involve your name or initials in some capacity. One that you're not squeamish about giving out, because you want people to be able to contact you. Mine is Stephanie@StephanieMorrill.com. On Twitter I'm StephMorrill. You're building you and your brand, and you don't want your brand to involve the TV show you love or the band you obsess over.

This goes for writing organizations too. I taught at a teen writer conference that has an online forum. The whole weekend, I would hear the writers say things to each other like, "You're PunkRockGirl? Oh! I'm BallerinaJane." There's nothing wrong with that at all, but my point is that they were so used to each other's handles, they didn't even know the real names of the people they were talking to on a daily basis. So if you're trying to put yourself out there in the industry, be sure to use your name.

Guideline #3
Like it or not—grammar matters

Ever since the ink dried on my signed contract, I've had people asking me if I would take a look at their manuscript. I almost always say no, but sometimes it's easier than others. Especially when I get an email that says things like:

> Ms. Morrel,
> i have attatched the first chapter of my book for you to look at. can you do it this week????? you might not undertstand some fo the plot stuff but its a fasinating story. write me back as apap. i really want to get published!!!!!

If someone doesn't know where all the commas go, that's one thing. But if she hasn't taken the time to spellcheck, or if she didn't bother with something basic like capitalization, my assumption is she hasn't taken the time to do so in her manuscript either.

Agents, editors, and professional writers are super busy people. If you want one to invest time in you, put your best foot forward.

Guideline #4
Don't act entitled

This is a tough line to walk, because you certainly don't want to put yourself out there as The Next Big Thing . . . but you also don't want to be like, "I've attached my manuscript, which isn't perfect and probably still needs a lot of work."

Let your story stand on its own merits. Describe who you are and what your story is about without injecting your opinion of it. Or your grandma's glowing endorsement.

It's also important to be respectful that the professional you've contacted probably has many other things going on. Professional writers have their own writing to attend to, agents have clients to service and deals to make, and editors have authors and deadlines and manuscripts to edit and all kinds of stuff. This is why you always send a query letter or email asking if it's okay to send your stuff. (We'll get to query letters in Chapter 24.) This is also why you should always:

Guideline #5
Say Thank You

Who doesn't like being thanked for stuff? You don't have to get ridiculous with it, but a simple, "Thank you for your time and consideration," at the end of your email can make a big difference.

I also recommend it for when you receive rejections. Again, a quick "Thank you for your time and consideration" is all that's needed. Not only is it a rare kindness, but it's a great way of releasing the rejection's hold on you.

Honest criticism is hard to take, particularly from a relative, a friend, an acquaintance, or a stranger.
—Franklin P. Jones

19 Critique Groups

by Jill

If you want to become a better writer, if you've written something and want an opinion on it, or if you feel your piece is ready for publication, it's a good idea to get some feedback before you submit to a publisher. And not just from your best friends and family, either. At some point, you need to find a serious critique group.

How to Find a Critique Group

Libraries often know of local writers' groups where you can meet people and form a critique group. Also, professional organizations like Romance Writers of America or the Society of Children's Book Writers and Illustrators have local chapters that make it easier to find other writers.

Because I live in a very small town, I have no access to in-person groups. So I use online critique groups. These are good because I can read and post from home at my convenience. You can easily find hundreds of critique groups by doing a Google search. Simply type in your genre and the words "critique group" and you'll get lots of options. For example: science fiction critique group. You can also find online critique groups through professional organizations like I mentioned with in-person groups.

Not every critique group is a good fit. You might join some only to quit shortly after. That's okay. It's important that you find the right group for you.

A Note from Jill
About Professional Organizations

A great way to meet other writers is to join a professional organization for writers. There are hundreds, and you don't have to join them all. I'm a member of three: two national and one state. Here's a short list of national organizations that I recommend, but be sure and look for ones in your state as well, since that will help you find other writers that live near you.

Academy of American Poets: www.poets.org
American Christian Fiction Writers: www.acfw.com
Association of Christian Writers in the UK:
　　www.christianwriters.org.uk
American Crime Writers League: www.acwl.org
Australian Society of Authors: www.asauthors.org
British Crime Writers' Association: www.thecwa.co.uk
Canadian Authors Association: www.canauthors.org
Canadian Society of Children's Authors, Illustrators, and
　　Performers: www.canscaip.org
Christian Writers Guild: www.christianwritersguild.com
Crime Writers of Canada: www.crimewriterscanada.com
Fellowship of Australian Writers: www.writers.asn.au
Fiction Writers Connection: www.fictionwriters.com
Historical Novel Society: historicalnovelsociety.org
Horror Writers Association: www.horror.org
Military Writers Society of America: www.mwsadispatches.com
Mystery Writers of America: www.mysterywriters.org
Poets & Writers: www.pw.org
Poetry Society of America: www.poetrysociety.org
Romance Writers of America: www.rwa.org
Science Fiction & Fantasy Writers of America: www.sfwa.org
Sisters in Crime: www.sistersincrime.org
Society of Children's Writers and Illustrators: www.scbwi.org
Western Writers of America: westernwriters.org

What to Expect

Whether you're in an in-person group or an online one, expect to share one chapter of your work at a time. An in-person group might pass the chapter from person to person so everyone gets a chance to read it. In an online group, you might post your chapter so that people could download it to edit.

If you don't ask for specific help, critique partners tend to point out anything and everything that they feel is a mistake or could use improvement. So it's always a good idea to decide what kind of help you want before you share your manuscript. This will solve a lot of problems before they start.

Beware of the critique partner who is a new writer but thinks she knows everything and is always right. This type of person is rarely helpful. Look for critique partners who are humble. They will be the best fit. And stay humble yourself!

You don't have to take every bit of advice you get, but it's good to know what people are thinking. This is part of the learning process.

Here are a few things you can do before submitting your work for critique.

1. Decide what you'd like your critique group to look for. Do you want a full line edit? Or do you simply want to know if the story holds their interest?

2. Check for grammar and spelling errors. The spellcheck is great, but it doesn't catch mistakes like: its/it's or their/there/they're. Train your eye to catch these things before you ask others to look over your manuscript. Always be as professional as possible.

3. Make sure that your manuscript is formatted correctly. One inch margins all around. Double spaced. Times New Roman 12 point font.

4. Prepare yourself for criticism. Your critique group doesn't want to hurt your feelings. They're trying to help you improve what you've written and want the same help from you. Be ready for that. When you're waiting for your feedback, you might want to psych yourself up a bit because taking criticism can be hard. Try to keep in mind that all writers are criticized. Even bestselling authors get

negative reviews. It's part of being a writer. A critique group is a great place to start getting used to it.

Also remember that a critique group should be a safe place to learn. Expect negative feedback, and try to embrace it as an opportunity to make the story better before you send it to a publisher. But if your critique group is hurtful and disrespectful, you should probably look for a new one. Try not to be overly sensitive, though. By its very nature, a critique looks for the negatives in your writing. Weaknesses and mistakes that we all make. No author is perfect. So it's logical that a critique group spends most of its time talking about what's wrong with your piece rather than what's right.

When you get your work back, read the comments over once rather quickly. If you're frustrated or angry, close the file or put the paper away and wait a day or two. Come back to it when you've had time to think and relax. Then, let it go. Sometimes you just have to agree to disagree. But if you find that three or more people have given you the same advice, you'd be wise to listen.

Things that Make Good Critique Groups

1. Have a leader, someone to organize and keep things moving so that no one person gets all the attention

2. Set up some rules for the members to follow. These could be: attendance, give a critique before receiving one, balancing negative feedback with positive feedback, members must write new material. Without some rules, you'll have no structure.

3. Meet regularly. Writers need to get used to writing consistently and meeting deadlines. A critique group is a great place to start this training.

How to Critique a Manuscript

One of the best ways to become a better writer is to learn how to critique the work of others. It can feel strange at first, especially when you can't seem to find anything negative to say.

Start out by asking the author what kind of critique he's looking for. He may want all the help he can get. He may simply want your overall impression. Try to give him exactly what he's asking for. This will save you time.

Even if he asks for the works, don't point out every single negative thing you can. Skip some. This kind of critique is rarely helpful because if you do all the hard work, he will never learn. Point out things once, and suggest that he make the change throughout the manuscript.

Here are ten tips for providing a good critique:

1. Read the chapter through without marking anything. This way you get the heart of the story. As you read, ask yourself these questions: Are you confused? Does the beginning hook you? Is it realistic? Are you bored? Do you like the characters? Is there a problem the main character is facing? Do you feel drawn into the story?

Write down these thoughts at the end of the chapter. Try to keep your comments positive and encouraging. Be sure to point out positives first, then negatives. You can be honest without being cruel. Instead of saying, "This is so boring!" say, "The first few pages could use some more action. The pace seems slow." It's always best to avoid using "you" in your statements. Saying "you" always sounds like a personal attack.

2. Go back and read the chapter again, this time stopping to make notes when thoughts come to you. Try to make positive and negative comments. Even if the story is horrible, you can always find something positive to say. The purpose of a critique group is to improve your writing through constructive criticism. But people have quit writing because of harsh critique partners. Unless the writer asked you to rip it to shreds, don't point out every little mistake. We all learn a little at a time, so overwhelming someone with nothing but red marks isn't necessary. Baby steps, you know?

3. Consider not using a red pen. Pick a friendlier color like blue or green. If you're using Track Changes, you can choose a color, but it never seems to show up the same on someone else's computer.

4. Mark misspellings, grammar errors, and punctuation mistakes, but only if you're certain you know the correct rule.

5. Word use. Does the writer use too many passive verbs (be, is,

are, was, were). Advise him to use action verbs instead. Does he always use vague or bland words (walked)? Suggest he use more specific words here and there (inched, jogged, sprinted, loped, strode). Note where the writer's words stood out, good or bad. If a metaphor confused you or impressed you, say so. Point out when you didn't understand the description or when it hooked you into the story.

6. Dialogue. Does it sound realistic? Do character conversations move the plot forward? Does the author use too many said tags or action tags? Not enough? Is the punctuation correct?

7. Viewpoints. Can you understand the point of view? Are the transitions from one point of view to another smooth and clear?

8. Did the author use the proper manuscript format? We should all get in the habit of writing in the industry standard format at all times.

9. When you finish, edit and proofread your critique to make sure it's clear, kind, and doesn't contain typos.

10. Remember whose story it is. He doesn't have to accept your advice. Be careful not to critique personal preferences. We are all different. We don't want to critique each other to the point that we strip the personality from each other's writing. Our unique way of saying things is part of our budding voice. So don't squash that out of each other.

I always try to end my critiques with a statement like this: "These are just my opinions. Take what you like and throw out the rest."

When you give your critique back to the author, let it go. And don't be offended if he chooses to ignore some or all of your suggestions. The point of a critique is to give your honest opinions and advice. What the writer does with that information is up to him.

Sometimes the Group is Wrong for You

One of the first critiques I got on my manuscript wasn't helpful. And it caused me a lot of confusion. The person reading it didn't understand YA fiction. She clearly didn't read YA fiction, either. Her remarks were negative and hurtful. She shamed me for writing about teenagers who got into fights and told lies.

Thankfully I only doubted myself for a week before I realized what really happened.

She wasn't one of my target readers.

Finding a good critique group or even a single critique partner isn't easy. Look for someone with similar goals and needs as yours.

When I first looked for a critique group, I couldn't find a local one. So I went online and found a group that had every genre and every level of writer. I got some good critiques there, but I also found a lot more people who didn't understand my genre. One of the writers in the online group who wrote YA, Diana Sharples, and I vented to each other about this. I remember emailing her a comment: Someone should start an online critique group just for YA.

The next time I checked my email, Diana sent me an invite to an online YA critique group. She and I were in that group for many years. It was a fabulous group. We all learned a lot from each other, and many of us are now published.

Once I got published, though, my needs changed. Suddenly I had deadlines. And I needed critique partners who could read my entire story quickly rather than one chapter a week. So I found partners to trade manuscripts with, rather than a large group.

Critique partners matter, so don't skip this step. Work hard at finding at least one person who will ask the right questions and point out plot holes and inconsistencies in your characters because the good critique partners can make all the difference in getting your manuscript ready for publication.

Publishing is a business. Writing may be art, but publishing, when all is said and done, comes down to dollars.
–Nicholas Sparks

20 The Publishing Industry Decoded

About Traditional Publishing
by Jill

Most writers dream of getting published, but few know how to navigate the challenging process to get to such a point.

What goes on over at those publishing houses, anyway? Why does it take so long to get an answer? Let's take a closer look at what has to happen to get your beloved novel in print.

First, you must have an incredible, flawless manuscript. This is no easy task and can take many years. But once you've reached that point, you're ready to submit.

To get published, you must get an **acquisitions editor** to like your book. An acquisitions editor is a person who works for a publishing house and is responsible for finding books to publish. Getting your manuscript to an acquisitions editor can be achieved several ways.

1. Send it to the editor at the publishing house.
2. Query an editor.
3. Pitch it to an editor at a writers conference.
4. Enter a contest in which an editor is a judge.
5. Have your agent submit your novel to the editor.

Most traditional publishing houses will not accept an unsolicited manuscript, which is a manuscript the editor did not ask you to send. It's like showing up to a party uninvited. The host says, "Who invited you?" and you say, "I invited myself."

Get the picture?

Traditional publishers don't accept unsolicited manuscripts because they just can't look at that many manuscripts. It takes too much time, and they don't have the staff to do it. Many publishing houses will accept a query letter, however. This is a one page letter that pitches your story to the editor in hopes of snagging her interest. (We'll learn how to write them in Chapter 24.)

But let's dream a bit. Let's pretend that you have an agent. Sweet, huh? You and your agent have worked hard to get your book and book proposal perfected. Now she's ready to submit your proposal to an editor. She'll likely send a quick email to tell you, "Just submitted your proposal to Tom over at ABC Publishers. Now we'll wait and see what he says!"

What happens next depends on the publishing house. Some houses are really slow. Some move faster. So you might get an update from your agent in a few weeks, or you might not hear anything for many months.

Meanwhile, here's what Tom is up to over at ABC Publishers. As the young adult editor at ABC, he works from seven in the morning to about eight at night. He's on salary, so there's no overtime pay. He works on about twenty-five books in a year. Today he's working on a content edit for one title, slogging through some more pages of a line edit on another, he's got a meeting with a cover designer to give feedback on a reprint cover, he's got to talk to Rachel in marketing about a book trailer, he needs to call the publicist in New York to talk out some ideas one of his authors has for promoting her book, he has a meeting with his boss (the publisher) to touch base, and he has 356 emails in his inbox, including some projects to reject, and he'd love to get his inbox to 300 before he goes home.

A few weeks later your agent calls to follow up. No, Tom hasn't had a chance to read your proposal yet but promises to try and get to it today.

When Tom finally gets a chance to read it, he LOVES it! He still needs a good fantasy project in next year's spring line, and this could be the book! He's so excited he puts the project on the agenda for the next editorial board meeting. He doesn't have time to call your agent and let him know this, however. So you don't know either!

But Tom does bring your proposal to the next editorial board meeting. At ABC, this meeting is made up of four people: Tom, the YA editor; Sue, the children's editor; Kathy, the middle grade editor; and Mike, **the editorial director**, a guy in charge of all the editors. Even though each of these editors is responsible for different things, they work as a team when they develop the ABC children's line. In this meeting Tom will pitch your project to the other editors. If they hate it, they'll say so. And if Tom can't get the editorial board excited about your book, he likely won't take it any further. Your book might be rejected here.

Here's a sample conversation from the editorial meeting after Tom presented your book to the team:

> **Kathy (middle grade):** I love it. But the premise sounds younger. Maybe you should send it to me.
>
> **Mike (editorial director):** Tom, you think this should maybe be a middle grade project?
>
> **Tom:** No. I want this one for YA. I think it has great appeal for an older reader.
>
> **Sue (children's):** My concern is that this is a new author. You're so busy right now. Do you have time to work with a new author? You know how they can be.
>
> **Tom:** I love this project so much it will be worth the extra effort. I'll work on it from home if I have to.
>
> **Mike (editorial director):** Wow, okay. Who's the agent?
>
> **Tom:** Melanie Smith.
>
> **Mike (editorial director):** Good! Melanie's great. She wouldn't send us someone who couldn't follow through.

The editorial board likes the project, so Tom makes a note to include your book in the next pub board meeting and puts the whole thing out of his mind. He's got a lot to do, after all.

Since the pub board—publishing board—only meets once a month at ABC Publishers, the next time your agent follows up, she learns that Tom intends to present your proposal there. Tom tells your agent how much he loves the project and is hoping it will fill that last publishing slot in the spring line. Your agent emails you to relay this information.

Not Many Publishing Slots

The problem is that every house has a limited number of books that they publish each year. Some may only publish five books a year, some thirty. Of those, most of the slots are for the house's established authors. If you submit to a house that publishes Stephen King, he may have two of those thirty novel slots. The other slots are taken up with a host of other successful authors. The pub board will always fill the book slots with their well-known authors first. This only leaves a handful, maybe one or two slots for new authors each year.

Your book is going to pub board! You're doing a happy dance. You want to tell everyone and their cat, but you hold back. There's still a long way to go.

Things are still crazy over at ABC, so crazy, in fact, that the next pub board meeting got pushed back two weeks to deal with a crisis from a bestselling author who demanded a six-month extension on a book that's already pre-sold 200,000 copies. It's "all hands on deck" at ABC to fix this thing. Thankfully, Tom is not the editor working with this bestselling prima donna, but he still gets drawn into the drama.

Eventually, the rescheduled pub board meeting rolls around. This meeting takes place in a long room at a big table with chairs all around it and a lot of snacks in the center. Since ABC Publishers is a smaller house, there are only ten people present. The **publisher** (boss), the editorial team (Tom, Sue, Kathy, and Mike), the **sales director**, his **top sales rep**, the **marketing director,** Rachel, her assistant, and **the finance director.**

Here Tom gets his (and your) big chance. He spent a few hours preparing a video presentation to illustrate your project to the pub board. Mike tells everyone that Tom is going to present a young adult fantasy novel by a new author and that the editorial board thinks this could fill that last slot for spring.

Sales director: I think this one is great. It's got a *Percy Jackson* meets *Hunger Games* vibe that I can totally sell.

Publisher: I still don't understand what a crowl is.

Marketing director: Offspring of the gods and an elf. Think Galadriel.

Publisher: So it's Lord of the Rings meets Percy Jackson meets *Hunger Games*?

Sales: I like adding Tolkien. That will tie in with the Hobbit movies.

Publisher: But didn't *Percy Jackson* do the Greek god thing to death? Can we sell Greek gods anymore?

Marketing director: This one isn't Greek gods. They're crowls, which are Greek-like gods set in a fantasy world.

Sales director: I can sell anything I can relate to the Hobbit right now, you bet.

Publisher: Okay, Tom, tell us about these crowls.

Everyone is silent as Tom shares your plot in pictures, almost how a book trailer might look, though Tom narrates the story himself. He also presents the profit and loss statement and talks about sales figures for similar titles, how you have a YouTube channel where you post humorous video book reviews and have a huge following, and how he thinks you would be a great author for ABC.

Publisher: And you want this for spring of next year? You think a new author can turn around the edits that fast?

Tom: Yes. And I'm willing to put in the extra time to make it work.

Mike: The manuscript is done. And the writing is great.

Finance director: But it's a lot to invest on an unproven novelist. Can you really sell twenty thousand copies on a new author?

Sales: With the Hobbit angle, I can sell fifty.

Finance director: *snorts* Sure you can.

Publisher: I still don't understand what a crowl is. It sounds like crone, and what teen wants to read about old ladies?

Sales: A crowl is the new hobbit.

Marketing: A crowl is nothing like a hobbit.

Sales: It is if I say it is.

Marketing: Whatever.

Mike: Well? Do we make an offer on this one?

Finance: Cut that advance in half and I say yes.

Sales: I say yes. I've been looking for a Hobbit angle to sell.

Marketing director: I vote yes. It's clever and smart, but accessible.

Publisher: It's not my kind of book, but I didn't like vampires or the dystopian craze, either, so I trust your judgment, Mike. And if we can sell twenty-five at the lower advance, I'll go for it.

And so you get an email or phone call from your agent with an official offer from the publisher! The offer might look like this:

Rights:
1. World English language rights
2. All international language rights, worldwide
3. All electronic/digital and ebook rights to the text of the book
4. Non-dramatic audio rights, both on a hard medium (such as a CD) and digital audio download rights
5. DVD curriculum rights

Advance: $5,000 ($2,500 payable on the receipt of signed contract, $2,500 payable on acceptance of manuscript)

Royalty: 15% of net.

Format: Softcover, $9.99, approximately 300 pages

Here you might bring up your concerns with your agent over the advance or when the manuscript is due. Your agent will negotiate this with the editor, and, once she's done, she'll email you a copy of the book contract. You'll read this carefully, ask your agent any questions you have, and when you're done, print three copies, sign each contract, initial each page, and mail them off to the publisher, who will process them, keep a copy for themselves, mail one back to you and the other to your agent. Sometime later, you'll receive the first half of your advance payment in the mail, minus your agent's 15%.

But what happens now?

Even though your manuscript was complete when you submitted it, you now have a delivery date to officially turn it in, and Tom asked for a few story changes in the contract, so you make those changes then go through the manuscript once more to make everything perfect. Once you officially turn it in, you have nothing to do but wait. You tell people you're having a book published. You start writing another book. But you've got to wait your turn for Tom to get to you again, because remember, he's a busy guy.

Eventually you get an email from the marketing director asking you to fill out a marketing information sheet. This asks for your author bio, how you'd describe your book, other possible titles, what you'd like on the cover, names of authors you'd like to get endorsements from, names and addresses of people you'd like to get a free copy of the book to review, names of your local newspapers and TV studios . . . things like that.

A few months later you get an email from Tom explaining that they've changed the title to *The Crowl*. You don't love this, so you email your agent for help. Your agent gets involved to express your concerns, but in the end, the publisher is too excited about a tie-in with *The Hobbit*, so you lose out.

A month later you get an email with your cover art attached. Other than the title, you love it. Whew! At least you don't have to complain again. You're really trying to be an easy-going author.

A few weeks later the marketing people email you a link to a book trailer they made for your book.

It's ah-some!

Then, while you're on your summer vacation and hop online at a computer in the hotel lobby, there's an email from Tom with your edits. He wants them back in two weeks, and you won't be home for three more days! You shoot off a quick email to let him know where you are, then open the edits really quickly to see how they look. You see a lot of changes! This depresses you for the last three days of your vacation, but you get home and see that they're not so bad after all. You spend all day, every day, of the next eleven days getting your edits done and turned in on time. Then you wait some more.

The edits go back and forth between you and Tom a few more times before you're both happy with the manuscript. You don't hear anything for a while until you get a PDF galley of the final book to read for mistakes. This file looks like a book! Your name is at the top of every even page and the title is at the top of every odd page. You ask your critique partner and your best friend to read the PDF too. You make a list of any errors and email that back to Tom.

More waiting.

Then one day you receive a package with an advanced reader copy inside! It's your book! It's beautiful. You laugh and cry and dance and show everyone in town.

You start to get emails from the publicist, who forwards you reviews from *Publisher's Weekly, School Library Journal, Kirkus, VOYA*, and, if you're lucky, an endorsement from a well-known author. The reviews are mixed. Some love the book. A few hate it.

Sigh. Such is life.

Meanwhile, you've been trying to learn the ropes of self-promotion and have set up a release-day book signing at your local Barnes and Noble. You've invited all your friends and family. You get a box with your author copies of the final book and you have your friend video tape the moment and post it to YouTube. That night you sleep with a copy of your book under your pillow.

Bliss.

Your book is now showing up for pre-order on Amazon.com, BarnesandNoble.com, and other online retailers! You pre-order a copy from every store, just for fun.

Release day arrives! The book goes live online and you spend the morning watching the Amazon rankings go up, hoping that everyone who promised to buy a copy will. That night you head over to your book release signing. Your friends and family are there to support you. Your mom buys ten copies. Your family and friends all buy one, but you're most excited about the three people who were actual customers who walked by, asked what all the excitement was about, and bought a book. You're hoping they'll become fans and buy book two when it comes out!

So there you have it. Pretty cool, huh? All this takes about a year and a half from submission to the book being available in stores. And that's much faster than it used to be. Still, if you'd taken a year or two to write that book, to rewrite it over and over, to edit it, find your agent, then work on the book with your agent, we're talking three years of work with no pay. You've got to really love writing to put in that kind of effort.

How Advances Work

Now that you're getting a big advance, you're finally going to make some money, right?

Not quite.

As per the scenario for the amazing novel *The Crowl* getting published, ABC publishers gave you a $5,000 advance on the book. Think of this advance as a loan. It would be like your boss down at Subway giving you a year's salary in advance. You'd still need to work to pay it back, but you'd get the money ahead of time—in advance.

This is not something you have to pay back. But it's an amount that you must reach if you are ever going to earn a penny more from your publisher on your book.

Your book advance is calculated on how many copies the publisher thinks they can sell. And once your book comes out, you must sell enough copies at your royalty rates that add up to $5,000 before you make any more money on your book. This is called "breaking even" or "earning out" your advance. Sadly, the majority of authors don't ever break even. In fact, many bestselling authors don't break even because they get such huge advances that the book never earns out.

That's why I prefer smaller advances. My goal is always to break even in the first year, if I can help it, which I sometimes can't. But a smaller advance is easier to earn back and, I feel, gives me a better chance at looking like a success to my publisher.

Once you break even, then you'll start to receive more money on your book. You'll receive your royalty rate from your contract on all future sales, which was 15%.

Also, returns count against you. Every quarter you'll get a royalty statement. The first one might look something like this:

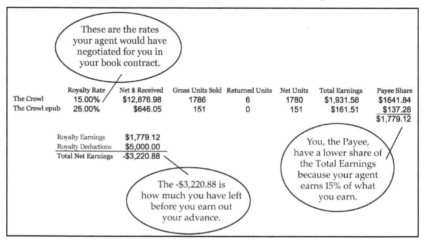

All this to say, the vast majority of authors need to have written multiple books that have earned out, are all still in print, and earning royalties before they can make a living. It adds up, but it takes time.

Something to Think About

If you have a favorite author, make a point of buying his or her books new, because authors don't make any royalties off used books or books you get free from their publisher. In fact, if you want to be an author, I suggest you make a point of buying at least one new book a month if you can. Because you know what it's like to be working hard to get published, and someday you're going to wish that someone would buy your book new.

And don't think that ebook piracy isn't a big deal. It is. Every ebook that someone emails to a friend without paying for it is another lost royalty for that hardworking, underpaid author.

Independent Publishers

Since it's so difficult to get published at a traditional house these days, many authors are starting out with small publishers. I did this. And it worked for me.

My first publisher did not pay an advance but offered a bigger royalty. He could do this because he used print-on-demand technology to produce the books. This means that a book is printed only when a customer orders one. This eliminates costs of large print runs where a traditional publisher might decide to print 5000 copies to start.

I worked very hard to market my book, and I did well. I got some nice reviews and won a few contests. I ended up writing a trilogy, which got me a small readership, an agent, and a publishing contract at a traditional house. Now I'm living the dream!

There are pros and cons to working with a small publisher.

Pros

•They need authors and your chances of getting published increase.

•You'll have a real book that you can promote and sell.

•You might make a higher royalty rate.

•A smaller advance or no advance means you make royalties sooner.

•They might not accept returns, so those won't count against your royalties.

•You might get answers quicker because the staff is much smaller than at a traditional house.

Cons

•The editor might not be as skilled as those who work in traditional publishing.

•The cover designers might not be as skilled as those who work in traditional publishing.

•Your book will likely be more expensive, since the publisher can't get quantity printing discounts.

•If the publisher doesn't accept returns, bookstores won't carry your book, which can limit how fast people find out your book exists.

•It might be more difficult to enter certain contests or get reviews.

•The publisher may have no marketing budget to help promote your book.

Never rush into any publishing deal. Take your time, consider the offer, consult a mentor or agent, and make sure you feel comfortable. It's your book! You want to make the best possible choice over which publisher to work with.

How to Tell if a Small Publisher is Legit

1. Are they going to charge you? If they are, they're a self-publishing company, not an independent press. You shouldn't have to pay a dime! And that also means that they should not ask you to contribute to the marketing costs, purchase any amount of author copies, or pay for editing services or writing classes.

2. Are they listed in the Writer's Market?

3. Are they listed at Preditors and Editors? www.pred-ed.com

4. Is their website professional?

5. What other books have they published? Research a few of the titles on Amazon.com. Do they have reviews? Read them to see what people liked and disliked.

6. Ask if they have wholesale distribution or if they sell books online only.

7. Jot down the title of one of those books. Visit your local bookstore and ask about ordering one. If the bookstore can't find the book in the computer, that's not good.

8. Ask how many copies they expect to sell in the first year.

9. Ask to speak with the person who will edit your book. Is that person excited to be working with you? What changes does he have in mind?

10. Read the contract carefully—get an agent or lawyer who knows publishing to help, if possible.

About Self-Publishing
by Jill

Self-publishing is when you pay a printer to publish your book. You also pay your own editor and cover designer. Some self-publishing companies will recommend editors and designers to you— I recommend finding your own experts, even if it costs more.

Two things I want to say about self-publishing:

1. You only get one chance to make a first impression.
2. Just because you can self-publish, doesn't mean you should.

Teens often throw out Christopher Paolini's name when this topic is broached. The fantasy novel *Eragon* was self-published in 2002 by Paolini International L.L.C., the publishing company Christopher's parents had already published three nonfiction books with. Chris had started writing at age fifteen, so he'd put in years of dedication into his craft by the time Paolini International L.L.C. published the book.

Financially backed by his parents, they went on a major tour to promote the book. Novelist Carl Hiaasen's son picked up a copy of *Eragon*, showed it to his dad, who eventually told Knopf about the book, which led to a major publishing deal.

The thing is, there are always one or two over-the-top success stories that motivate people. And that's good. But these kinds of success stories happen as often as someone wins the lottery. They're rare.

How many of you have parents who would quit their jobs, sell their house, and go on the road to promote your novel? Probably none. Nor should they! It's just too big of a financial risk.

Self-publishing used to be taboo. It was a sign of an author who'd cheated, skipped the hard work of learning to write, and paid to have his own book made. And while that's often still the case for many authors, self-publishing is not what it once was.

Times they are a-changin'.

In 1939, Robert de Graff founded Pocket Books, offering 25-cent

177

paperbacks in a world where the average hardcover book sold for $2.75. This revolutionized the publishing industry. Books could be cheap! That meant more readers, and over time, more money. Many publishers didn't think they'd sell. But boy did they ever.

While no one is exactly certain what was the first ebook published, people began reading them on their computers in the late 1990s. But it wasn't until Amazon released the Kindle in 2007 that reading ebooks became an entirely new type of experience. The Kindle wasn't the first ereader, but it made ebooks famous.

Little did publishers and authors know, the industry was about to change again in a big way.

Ebooks have also changed the face of self-publishing. It's free to publish your own ebook. And now Amazon CreateSpace allows people to publish print books for free too.

This can be dangerous. Because there are now thousands of writers self-publishing ebooks and print books, writers who aren't ready to be published. And buyers will not tolerate this for long. Because even .99 cents is too much to pay to read something filled with errors and no plot.

I'm not trying to be mean. I'm being realistic. Writing books is a business. It's also an art. Most people don't get good at anything without practice. So just because someone *can* self-publish an ebook—or a print book—it doesn't mean he *should*.

A person only gets one chance to have her first novel published. It's her name and reputation on the line. So make a good, smart, patient choice and wait until you're ready.

Now, there are many teens out there with self-published books. I've met dozens of them. Sweet kids with fun stories. And I'm not saying the fact that they self-published is a bad thing. I'm just saying it's TOUGH to sell those books, isn't it?

It's tough to sell any book.

I've never wanted to be a representative for Pampered Chef, Creative Memories, Avon, Mary Kay, etc., because I don't like selling things to people. And I hate only getting invited to someone's house because she wants me to buy something. I don't want the pressure of selling my own self-published book. I don't want to look at everyone I meet as a potential sale. It's just too stressful.

Self-publishing is best for people who have a speaking platform to sell their books. Say you survived a freak case of small pox and wrote your own harrowing tale. Medical groups across the country would be clamoring to have you speak at their summer retreats. So you self-publish your story and sell it on the back table. Because you have gigs—a place to sell your book—it makes sense to self-publish.

I strongly encourage unpublished writers to keep writing. To be patient. To practice, practice, practice and learn, learn, learn. Read books on how to be a better writer. Read books in your genre. Get involved in a critique group and learn what other people say about your writing. And save up and attend writers conferences. I've sold all my books at writers conferences so far. And writers conferences are the best place to show your writing to editors and agents who can give you feedback.

The better you get, the better book you'll write, the better chance you'll have of getting published by a traditional, royalty-paying publisher, the better chance you'll have of doing a whole lot of Snoopy dancing.

And when I see your book in print, I'll dance too.

Back in 2004 when I started writing, self-publishing wasn't what it is today. If it had been, I would have gone off and self-published my fantastical work of genius right then. I totally know I would have.

And that would have been a HUGE MISTAKE!

Here's the deal . . . I know self-publishing is tempting. You just want to hold your book. Have it to look at. Build some readers. To show to your friends and family. I get that. I was there.

But if you want to have a career as a novelist—if you're serious about this thing—then wait. I'm not kidding. At least wait until you've spent a few years trying it the regular way. Why? Because you need to put in the hard work of learning. If you don't, you cheat yourself of becoming a great writer.

You cheat yourself of the journey.

There are always exceptions. And if you've been hard at work for years, getting kind rejections from agents and publishers—or maybe you have an agent and the market just hasn't been right. Perhaps then it's time to self-publish. I have friends who've done this. And it's working for them. But this is after they learned to write a good book and another and another and another.

If you're going to self-publish, put up the money to get the help you need to do it right. I did.

I self-published a novella (*Chokepoint*) that tied in with one of my traditionally published teen books. I did it for charity, so I felt self-publishing was the best way to get the most money for my cause.

I found a professional cover designer. I paid a professional editor who was trained in editing fiction and who had references from authors I'd heard of. I paid an ebook designer to format the ebook right.

And I'm very proud of how it turned out.

If you're going to self-publish, do your homework. Don't ask your mom to be your editor, even if she has a PhD in English. Find industry trained editors who know how to edit story content as much as grammar and punctuation. Research them. Ask for references. Buy a book they've edited and read it. See for yourself.

But my advice to all of you will always be: Wait. Have patience. Work hard. Learn the craft. Write many books. Go to conferences. Submit your story to agents and editors. And wait. Becoming a traditionally published novelist is really hard work.

But it's SO worth the wait!

Step 3
Putting Yourself Out There

How we got started

Stephanie's story

I knew from first grade on that I wanted to write stories when I grew up.

And ten years later, when I finished my first novel, that was still basically all I knew—I wanted to write stories.

Which meant I needed a publisher . . . which meant they would need to see my story . . . ergo, I should just print off my manuscript and mail it to them. (I'm 100% serious—this really and truly was my thought process.)

But when I got online to find their addresses, I discovered a rather curious phrase on their websites—no unsolicited submissions. Oh . . . I couldn't just mail it to them?

So then I started looking for publishing houses—any houses—who accepted unsolicited manuscripts. I didn't pay attention to what kind of house they were, how their books were selling, or what genres they published. Honestly, I didn't even know what genre I wrote.

I found four. I printed off four copies of my 90-page manuscript, stuck it in an envelope with my SASE (self-addressed stamped envelope, another new term for me) and popped them in the mail.

Miraculously, two of them were kind enough to send me rejection letters.

Even more miraculously, one of them had actually *read* my manuscript. Like, the whole thing. The editor told me that for my age it was quite good, but that it lacked a strong ending. At the time, I was disappointed not to be getting published, but years later I see how amazing that response was. Not only was it a correct assessment, it's what made me dig into the industry a bit deeper.

I discovered genres, query letters, and literary agents. I quickly became so overwhelmed with how not-ready my manuscript was. This is when I became serious about writing a book that deserved to be published and about learning the ropes of the industry.

My parents and my boyfriend (who became my husband a few years later) were always really encouraging, but another person stands out to me from those days when I was fresh off my first rejections.

My senior English class had a tradition of every Friday, one person sat in the middle of the room, and we all took turns saying nice things about them, even the teacher. My turn came on the heels of that rejection. I'll never forget how Ms. Bromberg said, "Stevie, I know you've already received a rejection, but I fully believe that one day you'll be a published author." (Yes, because of a whim the first day of freshman year, I was known as Stevie during high school.)

I never got over Ms. Bromberg's words. And it was a joy to have lunch with her nine years later as Stephanie Morrill, multi-published author. Though she said to me, "If it's alright with you, I don't think I'll ever get over thinking of you as Stevie Hines."

Jill's Story

I had written half of a novel, and in my mind, I was ready to be published. So I started looking around to see how I was going to make this happen. My first plan was to gather a pile of books that were similar to mine. I figured that these might be the publishers willing to print my book. Once I had made a list of potential publishers, I looked them up in the *Writer's Market* and went online to check each publisher's submission guidelines. Here's what I found on every site: No unsolicited submissions.

Which meant, "Do not send us your manuscript unless we ask you to, which we won't because we have enough manuscripts to look through already. If you ignore this rule and send us your manuscript anyway, we will throw it in the trash. We will not notify you of this. You can plan on it happening. The only way we'll look at your manuscript is if your agent sends it to us."

Ouch.

Well, no big deal. I just needed an agent. So I picked up my *Writer's Market* book again and started making a list of potential agents. But guess what I found when I sought out each agency's submission guidelines?

No unsolicited submissions.

That's right. It was a conspiracy. So totally unfair.

But in all my research, I discovered a loophole.

The writers conference.

Writers conferences are events where writers come to learn from editors, agents, and published writers. These are opportunities to show editors and agents your manuscript despite the "No unsolicited submissions" rule.

I found a small, two-day conference in Anaheim, California and I went. I inhaled the information the speakers shared. And during one of the breaks, literary agent Steve Laube encouraged each of us to come up and give him our one-sentence pitch.

I had never heard of a one-sentence pitch until Steve Laube explained it, but I wasn't about to miss my chance to sell my half-complete work of genius to this agent. I just knew that when he heard the brilliance of my idea, he'd sign me on the spot.

And so I approached, Mr. Laube gave me the go ahead, and I began to speak. I said something like this:

"My story is about a teenage boy named Spencer. He plays basketball and eats peanut butter out of the jar. Anyway, he gets recruited by the Mission League to join this organization. And he thinks that's pretty dumb. But his grandma makes him go, or whatever, so he goes to Moscow with a bunch of other agents-in-training. Oh, and Spencer has these visions and dreams and stuff . . ."

You get the idea. Apparently I missed the part when Mr. Laube said to keep your pitch to *one sentence*.

Mr. Laube's eyes had glazed over long before he cut me off. He said something about teens not liking books about missionaries, that the young adult genre was pretty much non-existent, and that he didn't represent YA authors anyway.

Oh. Okay.

I went up to my hotel room that night and cried. Once I had got that out of my system, my brain kicked back in. Okay. Something had gone WAY wrong back there. I mean, I knew teens liked my story. And my story wasn't about missionaries, it was about spies. You know, *Mission League/Mission Impossible*? So, clearly I'd done a poor job explaining it.

And I supposed it might help if I finished the book. Duh.

I realized in that moment that I hadn't respected my new dream.

185

I'd known that I wanted to be a fashion designer since I was nine. I sewed daily, I subscribed to fashion magazines, I watched documentaries on famous designers, I went to a fashion design college, and I worked jobs in the industry. I knew my thing where fashion was concerned.

But writing? I'd spent six months writing half a book and expected to sell it for millions.

Yeah . . . it was pretty insulting.

So, I had a choice. Give up or keep at it.

I decided to keep at it.

Over the next four years, I learned everything I could about publishing and writing. I joined critique groups, I finished my book and rewrote it, I wrote more books, I read books on writing, and I had some articles published.

By the time I attended my next writers conference, I was ready.

And, by the way, one blunder with an agent doesn't seal your fate forever. Steve Laube and I are friendly acquaintances. I see him almost every year at writers conferences and we have fun talking about growing up in Alaska.

Hopefully, this section has prepared you for when you decide to put yourself out there.

How to Find a Writers Conference

There are all kinds of writers conferences. Google is the best way of finding them. Be sure to look for conferences that are right for your book. Don't sign up for the Romance Writers of America conference if you're writing a middle grade historical novel.

If you've never been to a writers conference, pick a small, local one for your first time, even if the right editors or agents won't be attending. You'll learn a lot. But if you're ready to pitch your book, look for conferences that have the right editors and agents there. The conference website will list the editors and agents under faculty and staff.

You can also look for writing organizations that you're part of to see if they're having a conference. Organizations like RWA (Romance Writers of America) and SCBWI (Society of Children's Book Writers and Illustrators) have their own conferences and so do many other organizations.

Why play the game if you don't swing for the fence?
—Blake Snyder

21 Preparing to Query

by Stephanie

While it's super tempting to send out query letters as soon as you type The End, let me tell you it's no fun trying to throw your book proposal together *after* an agent requests one. It leads to a night of scrambling around on the internet trying to figure out what the heck a synopsis is and how on earth you should write an author bio when the only credential to your name is being on the high school newspaper.

Before you send out a query letter, Jill and I suggest you know or have at least six things handy:

- Your genre
- Your target audience
- A hook for your book
- A paragraph description of your story, written in the style of back cover copy
- The first three chapters of your book—formatted correctly
- A synopsis

With all that information, you'll be putting together your book proposal. Let's talk about them in detail first.

Defining Your Genre
by Jill

Before you query or pitch your book in person, you need to define your genre. I struggled with genre when I first started out. I knew that I was writing for teens, but my first book had "weird" elements, and I wasn't certain where the book fit. It was an adventure story . . . but it was about spies too, which maybe made it a mystery. Yeah. That was it. I was writing a teen mystery. But what about the "weird" part? Did the "weird" make it paranormal, urban fantasy, or supernatural?

I didn't know. I agonized over what to write on my query letter or what to say when an editor asked, "What genre do you write?"

The thing is, there are so many genres out there. And if you can find your exact sub-genre, you'll have a better chance of selling your work and having your work stand out as unique in the market. Why? Because you're defining your target audience, and that helps an editor or agent know where your book might fit.

If you said, "This is a contemporary young adult novel." That can mean many things. It doesn't tell the editor or agent much about your book. And odds are, every teen alive won't like your story.

But if you said, "This is a contemporary novel about a teen swimmer." That's specific. And specific is the goal.

Here are some more examples:

"I've written a young adult medieval fantasy novel with a telepathy thread."

"I've written a contemporary science fiction/suspense novel for teens that deals with the subject of human cloning."

"I've written a young adult suspense novel about teen spies who fight supernatural beings."

"This young adult dystopian novel was inspired by the Babylonian exile from Jerusalem."

188

Make it Yours:

1. Think about what genres you would tag your book with. Historical? Contemporary? Sci-fi? Romance? Fantasy? Paranormal? If you're not sure, find books that are similar to yours and see how they've been classified.

2. Now try to come up with your unique twist to throw on the end. Is it a contemporary YA that confronts bullying? A fantasy novel with swords and technology?

Your Target Audience
by Jill

Another question an agent or editor might ask is, "Who is your target audience?"

If you're writing for teens, you might say, "Well, teens, of course."

But that's not the answer an agent or editor is looking for. And they really don't want to hear that your book is for everyone, because that's not possible. Marketing people need a demographic to target. And, really, there's no book out there that everyone likes.

If you can give the editor or agent a very specific reader, you will play into the sales and marketing side of things. The editor will perk up knowing that such things will please the sales guys at the pub board meetings.

Here are some examples of specific target audiences:

Guys who love HALO will connect with this book because it has a similar storyworld.

Empty-nesters will relate to my protagonist's youngest child leaving home.

189

My book targets young mothers who have small children and are frazzled.

Guys who love to hunt will relate to my character when he's lost in the woods and needs to find his own food.

Female athletes will really connect with the journey of my main character to make the varsity basketball team despite her hardship of having lost her father.

The same book could have another audience.

Girls who've lost their father will relate to my heroine's loss.

The point is, know who your target reader is and what he's looking for in a novel. Then communicate that to the editor or agent.

Your Hook Sentences
by Stephanie

In your proposal—or if you're planning to pitch your novel to an agent or editor in person—you'll need to be able to describe your book in just a sentence or two. And since you chose to write your story using 80,000 words, not 42 or 27 or 35, this can be incredibly difficult.

These go by multiple names—hooks, one-liners, one-line pitches, loglines (mostly for screenwriting), elevator pitches (refers to the oral version) and probably others that I don't know. We're going to call them hooks. Not only is it easier to type, it's descriptive of what you're trying to do with your one or two sentences.

It's helpful, I think, to start by thinking about the goal of a hook. The goal of your hook is to convey what your story is about in a way that stirs interest. Like if your friend says to you, "Do you want to join our book club? We're reading *Book You've Never Heard Of.*" Your response will likely be, "What's it about?

This is the moment you should keep in mind when you're writing your hook. The "What's it about?" moment. Your hook doesn't need to be strong *just* to convince an agent you've got what it takes to be a published author. Consider all the other ways your hook gets put to work:

Your newly-signed agent will be using it to sell your project. He or she will start calling up editors and saying, "I have this great project from a debut author. His book is about insert-the-hook-here."

The editor talks to other editors at the publishing house about it. "This book is great! It's about insert-the-hook-here."

The editor takes your book to the publishing committee to convince his coworkers that they want to buy this book, that's it'll be profitable. "What's it about?" they'll ask. And your editor will say, "Insert-the-hook-here."

Then the sales team will go out to their clients—the bookstores—and convince them to dedicate shelf space to this debut author. "His book is great! It's about insert-the-hook-here."

And then the bookstore employees will be selling the books to their clients using your hook. Even *you* will have another use for it. Like when you're sitting at a book signing and a person walks up to you, picks up your book and says, "You're the author?"

You'll straighten your shoulders and beam a smile their way. "Yes, I am!" The next words out of their mouth will then be, "So, what's your book about?" (Or they might instead read your own bio out loud to you in a slightly mocking tone, before putting it back on the table and asking where the bathroom is. True story. But most people at least feign interest in your book.)

Do you see how much bigger the hook is than simply taking up space on the book proposal?

Your hook needs to contain these five elements in as few words as possible:

Character
Conflict
Setting
Uniqueness
Action

Let's take a look at how this plays out in books that many of us are familiar with:

Harry Potter and the Sorcerer's Stone by J. K. Rowling: An abused orphaned boy discovers he's actually a celebrity wizard when he receives his invitation to attend wizarding school.

The Princess Diaries by Meg Cabot: An uncool teenage girl learns in the same week that she's failing Algebra . . . and she's the princess of a European country.

The Sisterhood of the Travelling Pants by Ann Brashares. Four friends discover a pair of jeans that magically fits them all, and it connects and empowers them when they are forced to spend the summer apart.

Another option for your hook is combining popular story ideas with settings or concepts. Such as:

Romeo and Juliet with vampires: Twilight

Gossip Girl set in the gilded age: The Luxe series

Teenage Superman: Smallville, which made a fortune pairing the perfect Superman with an imperfect teenager. (No offense, you teenagers, but I hope you can see how this makes it a great idea.)

Lawyers in trouble: John Grisham has made millions with this idea. Most lawyers lead a pretty dull life of paperwork, paperwork, and more paperwork, but not in Grisham's books.

Kid spies: This idea spawned Spy Kids, Agent Cody Banks, Alex Rider, Cherub: A division of MI6, and Jill Williamson's Mission League series.

(An aside: Sometimes this can be a wacky way to come up with book ideas—I'm convinced *Pride and Prejudice and Zombies* came from this tactic . . .)

These can be effective, particularly for an elevator pitch, but you'll still need to follow it up with your unique story details. So for *Twilight*, you could add, "A teenage girl falls in love with a vampire who doesn't kill people."

I love the way Blake Snyder (*Save the Cat*) describes effective loglines for movies. He says "it must bloom in your mind when you hear it. A whole movie must be implied, often including a time frame." And the same goes for the hooks in your proposal, they must imply a whole story, one that makes the hearer say, "Ooh, that sounds like something I'd like to read."

The Perfect Hook

There are lots of different ideologies about the perfect length and make up of a hook. Some will say it shouldn't be any more than twenty words. Some will say it should never include names. You won't please everyone, so it's best to stay flexible.

Also, some prefer the "tag line" style of hooks, like you see on movie posters or book covers. Like:

- •Save the world. Get the girl. Pass math. (*Agent Cody Banks*)
- •Sometimes the last person on earth you want to be with is the one person you can't be without. (*Pride and Prejudice*)
- •As darkness falls, the last dragon will choose its rider. (*Eragon*)
- •She didn't belong. She was misunderstood. And she would change him forever. (*A Walk to Remember*)
- •One ring to rule them all. (The Lord of the Rings)
- •Don't go near the water. (*Jaws*)
- •One choice can transform you. (*Divergent*, Veronica Roth)
- •It gives life. It deals death. It watches all. This prison is alive. (*Incarceron*, Catherine Fisher)

193

Your Back Cover Copy
by Stephanie

Like a hook sentence, your back cover copy is a tool for selling your book. First to agents and editors, but then to readers.

When people are perusing a bookstore, they'll flip the book over to read what your book is about. Or when you're being interviewed on blogs or in magazines, they'll often print the back cover copy. Also, when you're on TV, they use your back cover copy to explain your book to the audience.

The qualities of a good book blurb are similar to the qualities of a good hook. Your back cover copy should include:

Character: Who is the main character? Who is this story about?
Setting: Where and when does it take place?
Conflict: What are they trying to achieve? Why are they on this journey?
Action: How do they go about doing this?
Uniqueness: Why is this book different? Why should I invest the time in reading it?
Mystery: Often phrased in a question at the end, this is the part of the back cover copy that triggers an itch in the reader's brain, that makes them scratch by starting to read.

And you need to do it as concisely as possible. But how do you boil your huge, beautiful masterpiece into just 150 to 200 words? These authors did it:

The Time Traveler's Wife by Audrey Niffenegger

A most untraditional love story, this is the celebrated tale of Henry DeTamble (CHARACTER), a dashing, adventuresome librarian who involuntarily travels through time (UNIQUENESS), and Clare Abshire (CHARACTER), an artist whose life takes a natural sequential course. (CONFLICT—they're on two different timelines) Henry and Clare's passionate affair endures across a sea of time and captures them (ACTION) in an impossibly romantic trap (MYSTERY) that tests the strength of fate and basks in the bonds of love.

That is a 66 word description of a very complicated book, and it's done beautifully. The one thing that's hard to nail down in this one is the setting, but the time travel thing makes it clear that we'll be jumping around a bit, so it works without that piece.

Incarceron by Catherine Fisher

Finn (CHARACTER) cannot remember his childhood. He cannot remember his life before Incarceron—a prison that has been sealed for centuries, where inmates live in cells, dilapidated cities, and unbounded wilderness. (SETTING) No one has ever escaped. (CONFLICT) But then he finds (ACTION) a crystal key and a girl named Claudia. (CHARACTER)

Claudia's father is the warden of Incarceron. And Claudia is about to become a kind of prisoner herself, doomed to an arranged marriage. If she helps Finn in his escape, she will need his help in return. But they don't realize that there is more to Incarceron than meets the eye. Escape (ACTION) will take their greatest courage and cost far more than they know . . . because Incarceron is alive. (MYSTERY)

And you can just write a big "unique" around the whole thing because of how creative that idea is.

Make it Yours:
Now it's your turn to try! Approach your back cover copy the same way you might a novel—don't worry about getting it perfect, zippy, and the correct length the first time, just get down something you can work with and then revise.

Your Author Bio
by Stephanie

When I first started writing bios for myself, I was convinced that I was doing it wrong. I guess I assumed that when you reached the level of professionalism that requires a bio, "your people" did it for you.

Nope.

Talking about myself in third person felt awkward and listing my accomplishments seemed wrong, but bios are necessary and a well-written one is an asset.

Let's start with a few pointers. Bios should be written in third person, especially if this is something you're putting in your book proposal. If it's on your website or blog, first person can work fine, but you still might want to have a traditional one somewhere online to help out those who are looking for something to copy and paste into an interview.

Your bio should reflect who you are and why you're qualified for whatever it is your bio is being applied to. By which I mean, why you're qualified to write your blog or write your manuscript or be speaking on such-and-such topic.

And this is where youth can be a drawback. Because—to put it frankly—you haven't really done much yet.

When I wrote my first bio, it was for my materials that I took to a conference to pitch *Me, Just Different*. I was 23, and my bio read:

Stephanie Morrill lives in Orlando, Florida. She is a member of ACFW.

I had to beat those agents away with a stick!

Just kidding.

But what do you say when you haven't done anything yet?

You write something that showcases your potential. Here are some thoughts on what you could include:

•What you write (your genre or brand of stories)

•Why you write it

•If you blog and where.

•Any special education you have that applies directly. (If you write books about World War II, then majoring in history at your university is applicable. If you write contemporaries, it's not.)

•Something that qualifies you to write this book. So if you're writing about missionaries in Africa and you were raised in Africa by missionaries, you should mention that.

•A few unique things you're passionate about.

•Any writing societies you're a part of, awards you've won, or articles you've had published.

So let's give that a try using my unpublished writer self:

Stephanie Morrill is passionate about quality Young Adult fiction, perhaps because her teen years aren't too far behind her. She's a member of ACFW and won the award for the best new writer at the Florida Christian Writers conference in 2007. She lives in Orlando, Florida and enjoys rocking out to songs about heartbreak, despite being happily married.

It's not a dream bio or anything, but it has far more personality than my original.

Let's do another example. My main character in *The Revised Life of Ellie Sweet* is a teen who aspires to be a novelist, but she writes historicals. Here's a bio I wrote for her:

Gabrielle Sweet lives in Visalia, California, though she often fantasizes about being born in a different time and place. This is probably why she writes medieval romances for teens. She is a member of American Fiction Writers and blogs obsessively about her journey as a young novelist. She's passionate about indie rock, novels with strong heroines, and lattes with the perfect amount of foam.

In that last sentence I could have said, "She likes music, reading, and coffee," but that doesn't tell you much about Gabrielle, because I bet in two minutes you can name 50 people who like music, reading, and coffee. This puts a unique twist on her tastes. Plus the "novels with strong heroines" part also communicates something you can expect from one of Gabrielle's manuscripts.

Hopefully this gives you an idea of what you can do with a bio when you don't have a ton of writing credentials to your name. Like all things writing related, if you want to get better at writing bios, it's a good idea to read lots of them. Surf the web for bios and see what connects with you and what doesn't.

Your Synopsis
by Stephanie

I know it's weird, but I adore writing synopses. I've taught classes on them, and I always feel like a bit of a kook standing up there saying, "You don't have to hate synopses! They can be fun!" (Though if somebody tried to convince me that writing hook sentences could be fun, I would totally give them the stink eye.)

One of the things I used to hate about synopses was having to condense my 75,000 word novel into two pages of summary. I used to do all this work going through my book, writing down what happened in each scene, and then trying to string it all together to make a synopsis. The result was always a stale, boring summary of my book.

Then—despite my stale synopses—I became a published author and the pitching process became different for me. Now I could sell projects *before* I wrote them . . . but they wanted some sample chapters and a synopsis.

I thought it was going to feel like torture. I thought there was no way I could churn out a decent synopsis for a book I hadn't even written yet.

Instead, it wasn't just the easiest synopsis I had ever written, it was the most fun I'd had writing one. It felt creative! I wasn't merely reciting details of my already-penned manuscript, I was creating. I was testing plot lines. I was envisioning the ending when I'd barely written two chapters. And not only was it more fun, the synopsis was super helpful when I wrote the book. When I got stuck, I could pull it out and get back on track.

So on your next project, if you're a seat-of-the-pants writer, consider writing a couple chapters, and then taking a break to write a synopsis. Even a rough one.

Jill is more of a plotter than I traditionally am, and she has a different way of putting together her synopses. When I asked about her method, she had this to say:

I write one sentence for each of the following things to create my one-paragraph blurb. I use this blurb in my query and cover letters.

1. The introduction, where the story starts
2. The hook at the end of Act One.
3. The big twist in the middle of the book.
4. The hook at the end of Act Two.
5. The climax and conclusion

Here's my five-sentence paragraph for *The New Recruit*:

(1) A teenage boy is forced to train in a Christian spy organization that he wants nothing to do with. (2) When he learns that his parents were also spies and that his dad betrayed his mom, he throws himself into being the best agent he can be. (3) He travels to Moscow on a training mission and discovers a connection between a Russian boy and a suspicious woman. (4) He witnesses the Russian boy sell information to the woman, betraying the local field office. (5) When our hero learns that the woman plans a final attempt to infiltrate the field office server, his only way to stop her forces him to draw near to the God who he feels abandoned him years ago.

Then, to write my synopsis, I take these five sentences and stretch each into a separate paragraph, adding more detail. This gives me a rough outline of my synopsis. I only need to add a bit more to make it flow nicely. I try to keep out most of the side characters and side plots so that I don't confuse the reader. I also learned at a writers conference, that it's a nice touch to put the character's name in all caps the first time you type it in a synopsis. (You can read Jill's synopsis for *The New Recruit* at the end of this chapter.)

Okay, so that's a bit about how Jill and I go about writing our synopses. Let's talk about some techniques for writing a good one.

Format it right

Synopses are almost always written in third person present tense. ("When Stephanie is done with work for the day, she turns off her computer and goes upstairs to play with her kids.") You *can* get creative with this . . . but you do so at your own risk. Be mindful of the synopses' purpose—communicating your story. Don't make your creativity so bedazzling that the editor or agent can't fish the story out of all that glitz.

Also, for whatever reason, synopses are always single spaced. If the agent or editor doesn't request a specific length, one to three pages is a safe guess.

Include Backstory

While in story writing it's best to sprinkle in backstory, with the synopsis, you often get to lead with it. When I write mine, the first paragraph is typically backstory and setting up the story premise.

Tell, don't show

Another way synopses differ from novel writing technique is the telling and showing rule. In a synopsis you should tell rather than show. Sentences like, "Stephanie is happy with the way she finishes up her day," would mark you as an amateur in a novel, but telling is the technique for writing a strong synopsis.

Start with your main character

I often see synopses that start with something like, "What would you do if all your friends turned into rabbits, and it was up to you to make them people again? That's precisely what happens in THE RABBIT FETCHER, a story about John Smith who . . ."

That's fine for a query letter, but in your synopsis it's better to start with something catchy about the main character. Like, "Much to his embarrassment, twelve-year-old John Smith has always been scared of rabbits."

Show off your voice

I suppose it's because synopses feel more like the technical manual to your novel than anything else, but many writers scrub their voice out of it, which makes it way drier than it should be. You want the synopsis to reflect the feel of the story. So if your story is funny, there should be hints of humor in your synopsis.

One of the best examples I've seen recently was in the synopsis of an unpublished friend of mine, Susie. In her romance novel, a group of old church ladies is trying to fix up the hero and heroine. But Susie doesn't call them a group of old church ladies, she calls them "the cupid committee." Her using that phrase tells you something about her story, doesn't it? (It also tells *me* that Susie won't be an unpublished writer for long.)

You can do this with sarcasm as well. If you have a character who's a bit snarky or sarcastic, make sure that comes through in your synopsis. Here's an example from one of mine:

Violet's only problem is—and she can't believe she considers this a problem—Cooper Thompson has done everything but pee on her to mark her as his. Violet used to think she was in love with Cooper, but in the last year she's seen a side of him she's not so crazy about.

We get a feel for Violet's sarcastic side.

Or if your synopsis is for a historical novel, throw in the occasional historical word or phrase. A little goes along way with this, but by swapping out, "It's a shame," for "'Tis a shame" you'll steep historical flavor into your synopsis.

Don't clutter it up with names

Deciding who gets named and who doesn't in a synopsis can be tricky because if you name too many, it's tough to follow. If you don't name enough, your story can feel shallow. Here are some rules I use for naming names when writing my synopsis:

•Main and primary characters often get first and last names used at the first mention. I just like the feel of it. I think it subtly communicates, "This character is a big deal."
•If a character is mentioned multiple times in the synopsis, or if he plays a big role in a twist in the story, first name only.
•If he only gets mentioned once in the synopsis, then I just call him by his relationship. (Her good friend, his teacher, his sister, etc.)

Don't tell the story in perfect chronological order

This has the feel of a chapter-by-chapter outline but without all the, "In chapter two," stuff. Unless the agent or editor has specifically asked for a chapter-by-chapter synopsis, that's not what you want.

Instead you want to sit on the various plot lines for a bit. So say throughout the story your character is having problems with her mother, but she's also having problems at work. (Your character likely has a lot more than two problems, but I'm sticking with two for simplicity's sake.) Maybe in the book the breakdown looks like this:

Chapter 10—Character learns Mom has boyfriend.
Chapter 11—At work, the character drops a milkshake on a customer but fortunately her boss isn't there.

Chapter 12—Character fights with Mom.

Chapter 13—At work, character's boss learned about milkshake and threatens to fire her if it happens again.

Chapter 14—Mom tells character that she's getting remarried.

Chapter 15—Character drops milkshake on customer again.

But in your synopsis, you'll group the mom stuff together, build it up to a tense point, and then cut away to the work stuff. It might look like this:

When Character learns her mom has been dating her biology teacher, she's furious. She's even more furious when she learns they're getting married. How could her mother do this to her? Meanwhile things are horrible at work. Character drops a milkshake on a customer, and even though her boss isn't there, he hears about it from a snitch coworker. He threatens Character that if there are any more shenanigans, she'll be hanging up her apron. And when a cute boy has Character flustered, and when she drops yet another milkshake on his lap, she fears the worst.

So even though those storylines alternate on-stage time in the book, in your synopsis you want to consolidate.

Tell Your Ending

This isn't the time to hold back plot twists or your fabulous ending. You want to divulge it all because the agent or editor is trying to gauge how well your story is crafted. I often end my synopses with the feeling the character is left with, and I noticed Jill did the same thing at the end of her one-page synopsis for *The New Recruit*.

The New Recruit
Synopsis

When two strangers appear on his front porch, SPENCER GARMOND is certain that GRANDMA ALICE GARMOND is sending him to military school for getting into too many fights. The men are Christian spies, however, who have come to recruit Spencer into their organization. He wants nothing to do with them, but Grandma Alice insists he accept his call to be a spy or enjoy life at military school.

Spencer reluctantly begins training. He makes a friend and an enemy among the other recruits, and struggles to fit in. An uncle he never knew tells him that his family has been spies for generations, including his parents. His dad sold out, and his treachery led to the death of Spencer's mother. Spencer vows to avenge his mother and works toward being the best agent ever.

He arrives in Moscow on a training mission. On a tour of the local field office, Spencer recognizes the face of a foreign woman on an assignment dossier. She has haunted his dreams for years. He prints out the paper on the woman named ANYA VSEVELODA, desperate to know who she is and why he dreamed about her.

Spencer befriends PASHA IVANOVICH, a homeless Russian boy, and notices Pasha's labyrinth tattoo. When Spencer sees Anya in a subway station, he follows her and discovers she has the same tattoo as Pasha.

Spencer's investigation leads him to a local Internet cafe where he learns about a cult called Bratva that uses the tattoo symbol for their logo. He visits Bratva headquarters to find out more and is nearly captured.

Spencer is furious when he witnesses Pasha selling information to Anya. Pasha betrayed his family like Spencer's dad betrayed his. He struggles to forgive his new friend.

Spencer finds out through conversations in a chat room that Anya plans a final attempt to infiltrate the field office server. His only way to stop her forces him to return to Bratva Headquarters and trust God who he feels abandoned him years ago.

Although Anya gets away, and Spencer is reprimanded for breaking protocol, his efforts provide valuable information into Bratva, and his experience draws him closer to God.

Before the Americans head back, a smug Anya approaches Spencer, bragging that he failed to stop her. She warns him that she knows who he is and who he is meant to become. She promises to make sure he fails.

The New Recruit is the first in a series of four novels about Spencer's experiences in the Mission League.

I love being a writer. What I don't love is the paperwork.
—Peter De Vries

22 Creating a Book Proposal

by Jill

Once you've figured out your genre, target audience, hook, back cover copy, and synopsis, you're well on your way to having your book proposal put together. What you include in your book proposal depends on who you're submitting to and what he wants to see, so it's good to stay flexible. Most houses and agencies have submission guidelines on their website or listed in a writer's market book. Follow their guidelines exactly. If there are no guidelines, here are some things you might include.

Overview

Here you'd give the title, word count, genre, target audience, hook sentence, and back cover copy. You'll want them in a format that an editor can glance at quickly, bullet points (when appropriate), and lots of white space.

You might also include a blurb about how your target readers will connect with your book's main character or what inspired your story. Here's mine from my proposal for *RoboTales*.

My son and I were talking books one day, and I told him we should write one together. We came up with the idea of writing fairytales for boys. The ideas were endless, as there are so many fairytales out there. But it wasn't until we came up with the title *RoboTales*, that we really got excited. Something fun, designed for boys, that could have both science fiction and fantasy elements, where the readers could gather clues in each story, learn something, and enjoy the adventure. And, of course, what boy doesn't love a robot dog?

Market Analysis and Competitive Titles

This is where you talk about the market and why your idea is timely. Include a list of books that are like yours, mention similar movies that have been popular, and any world events that may coincide with the release of your novel. If you have any well-known authors who've agreed to read your book for possible endorsement, list them in this area.

Synopsis

Stephanie went over how to write a synopsis in Chapter 21.

Chapter Summary

This isn't necessary, but some authors like to include a chapter summary. You simply list each chapter and give a one-paragraph synopsis. This often gives the editor or agent a more in-depth look at your overall story.

Character Profiles

This is something we've never done, but many authors include character profiles that give a one-paragraph glimpse into the goals and motivations of each character. This can help the editor or agent see how the characters will play off each other.

Author Information

In this section, put a short author bio, maybe a half-page long. Stephanie talked about writing author bios in Chapter 21. Make sure to list any published works. If you're a published novelist, you'll include sales information on each title here. If you've only published articles or short stories, you can list them. Here are a few of my entries:

"The Perfect Gift." Shine Brightly, December, 2007, pp. 16-17. ($35)
"Grieved." Devo'Zine, July/August, 2007, pp. 9. ($15)

You'll also include information about your platform here. List your websites, blogs, and their stats.

Marketing and Promotion

If you have marketing ideas for your book, you can put them in this section. They're not mandatory, but it certainly won't hurt you to add them. The more complete package you can hand the publishing house, the better chance you have of getting them to say yes.

You can also mention any connections you have, like friends who work for the news, radio, or the local newspapers. Don't worry if you don't have some of these things. Include what you can and leave the other things off. Especially for a debut author, the editor or agent will mostly focus on your writing.

I posted my book proposal for *Captives* on my website. Again, it's best to stay flexible because every agency and house seems to ask for different things, but it's helpful to at least see one proposal that did its job and landed a book deal. You'll find it at this link: http://www.jillwilliamson.com/teenage-authors/examples/

Endorsements

An endorsement is a short, positive review from a published author. Once you have a book contract, you want one of these if you can get one, but only from a well-known author in your genre. If you're writing science fiction (unless it's a science fiction romance) an endorsement from Janet Evanovich isn't what you want.

Brainstorm a list of potential endorsement candidates based on authors who write books similar to yours.

Start asking for endorsements as soon as you sign the contract. Most authors expect to get a year or so to read books for endorsement. Don't rush endorsers. You'll annoy them. If they agree to read your book, wait patiently. If you don't get the endorsement by the date you asked for it, you can send one, polite reminder email. And if they send the endorsement to you late, you can still use it, even if it's too late to go in the book.

If they never get back to you, don't think of it as a personal attack. Authors are busy. The mere fact that they tried to fit you in is a compliment. Be thankful. They also might not love your story. This happens. Don't keep emailing them and put them on the spot to find out.

After I signed my contract for *By Darkness Hid*, I emailed twelve authors for an endorsement. Five said yes. Three of those five actually wrote an endorsement for me. I never heard from the other two. Of the seven others, some said they'd love to but were too busy. One said he didn't like stories with telepathy and felt that his prejudice wouldn't be fair to me. A few never responded.

If you didn't get the endorsement in time for the book, what can you do with it?

-Post it on your Amazon page.
-Post it on your website.
-Add it to your press release.
-Add it to your promotional postcard or bookmark.

Wherever you post it, it can give your book instant credibility.

Here's the email I used to approach potential endorsers:

Mr. Author,

I recently contracted my medieval fantasy novel with Jeff Gerke at Marcher Lord Press. It will release April 1, 2009. I am seeking possible endorsement for the book. Since you also write fantasy novels, I decided to ask you. Here is the blurb for my novel, which is called *By Darkness Hid*, book one in the Blood of Kings series:

Blurb: Given the chance to train as a squire, kitchen servant Achan Cham hopes to pull himself out of his pitiful life and become a Kingsguard Knight. When Achan's owner learns of his training, he forces Achan to spar with the Crown Prince, more of a death sentence than an honor. As Achan struggles to serve the prince without being maimed, strange voices in his head cause him to fear he's going mad. He travels with a procession escorting the prince to a council presentation. Along the way, their convoy is attacked. Achan is wounded, arrested, and escapes from prison only to be brought back before the rulers of the land. There he discovers a secret about himself he never believed possible.

Would you consider reading the book for a possible endorsement? You can read a sample chapter to see if you like the writing style at this link: www.jillwilliamson.com/books/blood-of-kings-trilogy/by-darkness-hid-sample-chapter

Endorsements that are received by February 28, 2009 will be listed in the front of the book. If you are willing, I can send you an advanced reader copy or a .pdf copy.

Thanks for considering this.

Jill Williamson

Notice that I gave as much information as I could. The publisher and release date, a blurb, the date the publisher needs it by, and a link to sample chapters. I also was very polite and in no way assumed that they author would say yes. If you approach endorsements in this manner, you'll increase your chances of success.

A book proposal is your opportunity to make a sales pitch for your book. It's your chance to say everything you want to say to editors about why your book will be successful. Take the time to get everything just right.

Step 4
Finding a Good Literary Agent

A note from Stephanie

My search for an agent was time consuming, heartbreaking, and full of frustration. And it was a search for *an* agent. Not *the* agent. I was up for anyone who would take me on, and I think that's a normal feeling for an unpublished writer. When we're told again and again how hard it is to find an agent, it doesn't feel like we have any right to be picky. It feels like we should be grateful to whoever is willing to take a chance on us.

And even though I knew in my pre-agented days that a bad agent, or even an iffy agent, wasn't a good idea, I didn't fully understand how damaging it could be. Something I urge you to be mindful of is that literary agents have a reputation tied to them. It's a reputation that causes editors to either pick up their phones when that agent is calling them . . . or to let it go into voicemail. And whatever their reputation is, it affects you. (You can see how that plays out in Chapter 20 when the merits of *The Crowl* were being tossed around.)

I'm now represented by my first-choice agent. The second time around, I was smart enough to know to ask questions like:

•What kind of career guidance to you offer your clients?
•How many YA authors do you represent?
•Do you prefer to be contacted through email or the phone? How long should I expect to wait for a response?

But something I wish I had asked her during that initial phone conversation was what *her* goals are as an agent. What does she hope to accomplish? And what does she need from me for that to happen?

Understanding an agent's business philosophies and ambitions can help you to determine if this is indeed the right business relationship for you. I urge you to be patient. And though it's tempting to be desperate—I certainly was—I urge you to believe you're deserving of good representation, all the while continuing to grow your writing craft.

A note from Jill

An agent should be an author's helper. Someone who can do things the author cannot. Once you've written a few books, an agent is crucial. There's just too much going on to handle it all on your own. But new authors don't necessarily need an agent.

I know. I know. I didn't believe anyone when I started out. Everyone said, "Don't sign on with the first agent to come along." But I did. And my first agent was a good agent. He did a good job. But we were not the best match. And parting ways was very difficult for me. Plus, I didn't do the parting the way I should have. And it was really hard. I wish I could go back and do things better and smarter, but I can't.

So, please don't be in a hurry to get an agent! Get to know lots of people in the industry. Make friends. And when the time is right, you will find the right agent.

I did. And when I met the agent I have now, it was the perfect match. We get along very well. She gets me, she gets my genre, and best of all, she likes the weird books I write. What could be better?

When I finally find that one willing agent, I'll have found my prize in the Cracker Jack box.
—Richelle E. Goodrich

23 Literary Agents

Finding the Right One
by Jill

Because there are so many aspiring writers out there, there are lots of people who prey on their desire to be published, from vanity presses who pretend to be otherwise, to people who claim to be agents but have no credentials to their name.

You don't have to pay a dime until the agent makes a sale. A good agent will ask for 15% of your sales, no more, no less. You also don't have to sign the rights to your book away or anything like that.

Agents don't represent every type of book, so you need to seek out one who represents the type of book you've written. Here are some ways you can find agents and learn what he or she represents.

1. Buy a copy of the *Writer's Market* (or find one at your public library), and look through the agent section, making notes or highlighting the agents who deal in your genre. If you're writing for the Christian market, you need the *Christian Writer's Market Guide* instead. There is also a *Children's Writers and Illustrator's Market*. All these books are updated annually, so try and find the most recent copy you can.

2. Google something like "writers conference, looking for, YA horror" (or whatever your genre is). Sometimes writers conferences post which agents are attending and what they will be looking for. Google some variations of keywords until you get a nice list of names. Then you can Google those agents until you find their agency website and their submission guidelines. There might even be a receptionist you can whether the agent has plans to attend any writers conferences in the next year, but never call an agent directly! Calling an agent on the phone is a great way to never get an agent.

3. You can attend a writers conference and talk to agents there.

4. You can look at the acknowledgement section of books in your genre, and see if the author thanked their agent, then Google the agent's name.

5. You can ask your writer friends who their agent is, which is why I highly recommend joining some professional writers organizations, so you can start networking with other writers.

But don't expect your author friends to get their agent to like your book. All your friend can do is tell you who her agent is and maybe ask if her agent will take a look at your query. The decision is in the agent's hands alone. Don't sever author friendships because an agent rejects you. It's not your friend's fault.

Try not to be in a hurry. I know it's frustrating. You've worked really hard to complete that manuscript, and now you're ready to get connected and sell it. But the wrong agent can tie up your manuscript for years—or sell it to the wrong house. It's better to have no agent than to have a bad agent.

Make a list of the qualities you're looking for in an agent. Every author is different. We all want an agent who will sell our books, but even the best agents get rejections from publishers. So how do you know if the two of you might be a good fit?

Try and meet the agent first. It might be impossible, but there's a feeling you get when you meet someone face-to-face. It's an important thing to trust. Do you like the agent? Or does something about them bug you?

If an agent has offered to represent you, here are some things to consider:

1. Does the agent have the connections you need? Ask for a list of recent sales. Did those books come from publishers that your book might be right for? If not, it could be that this agent doesn't know the market for your book.

2. Ask for at least two clients he represents that you can email to ask for feedback on working with the agent. This is standard procedure and won't be seen as a rude request.

3. Ask about his process and what he does for his clients. Does he insist on helping edit your manuscript before he sends it out? Does he do career building? And do you want an agent who does these things or not? Every agent is different.

5. What kind of contract is he offering? Many agents have a thirty-day contract, which enables both parties to sever the relationship within thirty-days if one is unhappy. This is a nice thing because you're not locked into working with an agent for years.

6. If he's interested in your book, ask if he plans to represent only this book, or if he's interested in other books you have written or will write.

7. Does he communicate in a manner that works for you? Some agents are phone people. Some are email people. Many are way too busy to talk unless it's an emergency. If you're looking for a mentor in your agent, be sure and ask if he does that sort of thing.

I also wanted a female agent because I tend to have a difficult time working that closely with men. That's just one of my quirks. And more than anything, I wanted an agent who read my book and loved my writing. There are many agents who'll see that you can write and believe they can sell your book. And that's good. But you need an agent you can work with for a long time. Be patient. The time will come.

The Publishing Auction

One thing an agent can do for you that you can't do for yourself, is put your novel proposal on auction. This means that several publishers are interested in your book and willing to go to auction over the right to buy it. It's about the most exciting thing that can happen to an author. It happens mostly in the nonfiction market, so for a fiction book to go to auction is sort of rare.

Your agent would be the one who decides how to run the auction, and there are different methods of going about it. The author doesn't always choose the highest bidder. There's more than money to consider when signing a book contract, so the agent and author will look at the entire offer and choose the best.

This is every author's dream.

It's also every agent's dream.

> The essence of all great letters—all great writing—is the same: Energy, information, informality, and surprise.
>
> —John Wood

24 Query & Cover Letters

by Jill

When you get to the point of wanting to query an agent, you'll need a query letter as a means of introducing yourself. These days almost everything is done through email rather than snail mail. But how do you know? By reading the submission guidelines the agency or publishing house provides on their website, in a writer's market guide, or when an agent or editor extends an invitation.

Even though you're emailing, professionalism still matters. An email query or cover letter should be just as professional as a snail mail one. These are business letters to prospective employers and should be treated as such.

The Query Letter

A query letter is a one-page document introducing you and the story/article/book you have written. It's a sales pitch.

What agents and editors **don't** want to see in a query letter:

•More than one page! (If you think your email might be too long, type it in a word processing program first, then copy and paste into email.)

•The wrong name or misspelling of the agent or editor's name.
•Your life story.
•That your mom loves your book.
•A list of books you like and why.
•Your opinion of how great of a writer you think you are.
•How this is your first try writing and it was so easy.
•That you are the next J. K. Rowling.
•That God gave you this story, that it's His will that it get published, and they'll be sorry if they turn you down!

What they **do** want to see:

•One page!
•The editor or agent's name, spelled correctly.
•A professional and spell-checked letter.
•Your one-sentence hook or tag line.
•A back cover copy-type description of your project.
•Your word count.
•That your book is complete. (If it's fiction, don't bother sending a query if your book is not finished. You're not ready to sell your story until it has been finished and polished.)
•A small paragraph about you and your credentials.
•A reminder, if they met you and asked you to submit. (Agents and editors meet a lot of people. You can't expect them to remember every name, so a reminder is helpful.)
•A SASE or self-addressed stamped envelope (if you're mailing this query letter and want to know their answer.)

Try to stick to this format: A paragraph or two for the hook and book blurb, a paragraph for the information about yourself, and a closing paragraph. If you've met the agent or editor and have an inside joke, reference it. If not, stay professional. Here are some examples:

June 1, 2012
Susan Love, Editor
Romance Books R Us, Inc
100 Lovers Lane
Valentine, CA XOXOX

Dear Ms. Love,

What starts out as a bad day sends Katie Willis into the arms of the man of her dreams—or so she thinks. My novel, *Mysterious Stranger*, takes the reader on a wild ride of suspense, danger, and romance. It is complete at approximately 80,000 words.

Always in the wrong place at the wrong time, Katie Willis becomes a hostage in a bank robbery. Another hostage, Brooks Gibson, rescues her and they flee. The bank robbers want their eye witnesses out of the picture, however, and Katie and Brooks are forced to go on the run. As they journey toward the state line, Katie starts to fall for Brooks until events unfold that cause her to doubt his intentions. Could he be involved with the bad guys? Katie struggles to discover the true identity of this mysterious stranger.

I worked for six years as a vault supervisor for Bank of America, which gives me great insight about bank security. I am in two critique groups, one local and one online. Both groups have extensively critiqued my manuscript. I am a member of Romance Writers of America. *Mysterious Stranger* is my first novel.

Thank you for considering, *Mysterious Stranger*. I look forward to hearing from you.

Sincerely,

Beth Author

This letter is short and sweet. It starts out with a hook and informs the editor that the book is complete and how long it is.

Next Beth gives a tight, one-paragraph summary that leaves the editor hanging. It's good to do this in a query letter.

Then there's a short paragraph that includes mention of Beth's experience working at Bank of America. That's important. Since she's writing about a bank robbery, her work experience gives her first-hand knowledge of the inner-workings of a bank, which should make the story more believable. She also mentions a few of her writing activities, just enough to let the editor know that she's putting time into her writing career.

And she closes with a thank you.

When I was working as an editor, I would have been thrilled to receive such a concise letter, and I would have emailed the author back and asked for three sample chapters.

Here's the query letter for what became *By Darkness Hid*. I submitted this letter with a sample chapter to Jeff Gerke at a writers conference. Jeff published the book through Marcher Lord Press.

Dear Mr. Gerke:

Bloodvoicing is a gift, an endowment to communicate from one gifted mind to another. For a slave to have the gift is unheard of, yet one slave has more power than all the rest combined.

A young adult fantasy novel, *Prince Gidon* tells the story of two young people with a unique, ancestral ability to speak to, and hear, the minds of others: a slave forced to serve a prince who wants him dead and a young woman masquerading as a boy to avoid a forced marriage. The novel alternates between their points of view until their stories collide on the battlefield.

Judging from the steady stream of medieval fantasy novels on the bestseller lists, young adult readers remain fascinated by epic fantasy adventures. Projects similar to mine like *Eragon*, *Dragonspell*, *Chosen*, and *The Bark of the Bog Owl* bring a fun mixture of fantasy and faith to the Christian market.

I have two books contracted. *Jason Farms* will release in spring 2009 (a YA novel from The Wild Rose Press), and *A Mango and a Mud Church* will release in 2010 (an "all reader" book from Beacon Hill Press). My articles have appeared in *Brio*, *Brio & Beyond*, *Shine Brightly*, and *Devo'Zine*. My husband and I have worked with teens in the youth pastor role for nine years. I researched medieval life and swordsmanship for three months before writing this novel and can provide a works cited page.

If the premise appeals to you, I would be happy to meet with you to discuss the project. My agent, So and So at Such and Such Literary Agency, can provide a marketing proposal and the complete 96,000-word manuscript.

Sincerely,
Jill Williamson

When I met with Jeff, he told me this was one of the best query letters he'd seen. And what impressed him was my opening hook and how I smoothly went right into my case as to why my story would work in the current market. I'd written a compelling hook, and I had done my homework. If you do the same, you'll have an easier time getting an editor's interest.

The Cover Letter

A cover letter accompanies a submission to an agent or editor. It's not so much a pitch, as it is a reminder of who you are and why you are sending something. If an editor or agent responds to your query asking for sample chapters, you would send a cover letter along with them. If an author friend recommended you to her agent and the agent told you to email your manuscript, you would send a cover letter along too.

It's a good idea to put the hook from your query letter in the cover letter, in case the editor or agent doesn't remember or has never heard it.

The first example is a cover letter I wrote for an agent who requested my first three chapters. It's a bit long, but it worked for me. A month later, she requested the full.

Dear Ms. Chappel:

I enjoyed meeting with you at Mount Hermon Christian Writers Conference. I appreciate your willingness to review my proposal for *The New Recruit*, a young adult novel of approximately 80,000 words.

The New Recruit pits the powers of darkness against undercover agents working for God. Teens love action and adventure and have eaten up similar spy projects such as; Anthony Horowitz's Alex Rider Series, Frank Peretti's Veritas Project series, MGM's *Agent Cody Banks*, and Miramax's *Spy Kids*.

When two strangers appear on his front porch, Spencer Garmond is certain that his Grandma Alice is sending him to military school for getting into too many fights. The men are Christian spies, however, who have come to recruit Spencer into their organization. He wants nothing to do with them, but Grandma Alice insists he accept his . . .

... call to be a spy or enjoy life at military school.

Spencer travels to Moscow with other agents-in-training and stumbles onto a mysterious case. A local runaway betrayed the field office by selling information to a suspicious woman. When Spencer discovers the woman plans to infiltrate the field office database, he must stop her from exposing the secrets of his counter-cult organization.

My husband and I have worked with teens in the youth pastor role for eight years. I also run a website and critique group for teen authors. I participate in two online critique groups, both of which have extensively critiqued my manuscript. My work for teens has appeared in *Brio*, *Brio & Beyond*, *Shine Brightly*, and *Devo'Zine*.

Thank you for considering *The New Recruit*. I look forward to hearing from you.

Sincerely,
Jill Williamson

When that agent requested the full manuscript for *The New Recruit*, I sent a much shorter cover letter along with the book. She didn't need such a long reminder of who I was this time.

Dear Ms. Chappel:

Thanks for your interest in *The New Recruit*. I've enclosed the full manuscript for your review. Should you be interested, I can provide you with a marketing and series proposal.

I look forward to hearing from you.

Sincerely,

Jill Williamson

Work hard on your query and cover letters before you send them out. Have your critique partners help you. As long as you are clear and professional, you'll get the job done.

Good luck. Let us know what happens.

A rejection is nothing more than a necessary step in the pursuit of success.
–Bo Bennett

25 Dealing with Rejection

by Stephanie

Rejection is part of the writing life. Really, it's just part of LIFE. But since writing is a choice we make, when the rejection (or the fear of rejection) grows intense and strong, it's easy to think, "Why am I even doing this?!"

This is normal. All writers go through it. Even those writers you love and admire.

I encourage you to accept that rejection is part of this path. Try to view the rejections you get from agents and editors as preparation for mean-spirited Amazon reviews or bloggers who bash books for sport. Or for the really tough ones—the reviewers who offer criticism that you maybe, sorta, if-you're-being-100% honest, agree with.

When rejection comes—especially when you're just starting out—it's completely normal to feel like the victim of a drive-by shooting. The first time I queried literary agents, I was living in an apartment by myself. It's not too far from where I live now, and when I drive by there I always think about standing in the little mail room, ripping open the responses, then racing back to my apartment before I burst into tears.

In the beginning, I put a lot of pressure on myself to take rejection like a pro. To not let it bother me. Don't do that. It's okay to cry and be upset. Thick skin takes time to build and even now I'm not so sure how thick mine is.

When you get a rejection do not, whatever you do, write a nasty blog post about who rejected you or vent about it on Facebook. It's a bad, bad, *bad* idea. Agents and editors often Google authors who they're interested in working with. You do *not* want to be caught writing something nasty like that.

Instead, have a friend you can call when you hear bad news. This doesn't have to be a writer friend, but she does need to "get it." I've never discussed this with the person I call, but we have a silent agreement that in that initial conversation, WE are not the problem, nor is our book. THEY have the problem. THEY are short sighted. THEY just passed up a huge opportunity.

After whichever of us was rejected has cooled off a bit, we might allow that maybe, just maybe, the editor was right about a particular thing she said. But only that! The rest is hogwash! Oh, well, she *did* make kind of a good point when she said such-and-such . . . and how could we incorporate this suggestion into the manuscript, because that's really not a bad idea. In fact, hadn't we already decided that this character was a bit flat . . . ?

Those conversations are the best. I encourage you to build that kind of relationship with someone.

So if you can't blast the editor or agent on the internet, how *should* you respond when you get a rejection letter? Write them a thank you note. On real paper, with a real stamp, and all that good stuff. You tell them thank you for taking the time to look at your submission, thank you for the feedback (if they provided any), and you stick it in the mail within a day of the initial rejection.

This won't change their mind, of course, but it takes away the power the rejection has over you. I don't know the science behind that statement, but when I write my "Thanks for that great rejection!" notes, it feels like closure. I can breathe better after I drop it in the box.

Of course your rejection might be coming from a contest rather than an agent/editor. Back in 2008, I entered the first chapter of *Me, Just Different* in ACFW's Genesis contest. My judges were kind, but they were also honest. The biggest complaint was they hated Skylar. After a month of grumbling, I realized they were right. And without their criticism, I wouldn't have done my rewrite and *Me, Just Different* never would have been published.

This isn't to say that everything you read in a rejection letter is going to be good advice, so if something feels off or wrong to you, even after you've calmed down, it's fine to ignore it. As we've said elsewhere in the book, if you continue to hear the same feedback from readers, it's something you'll want to pay attention to.

Something else to remember as you wrestle with rejection is that agents, editors, contest judges, etc. are not rejecting *you*, just your book. I know how personal your projects feel because mine feel the same way. It's important to regularly remind yourself that they aren't calling *you* a self-absorbed brat, just your character.

When you get a rejection, or a particularly harsh critique from your writing group, don't be afraid to step back and indulge in something that recharges you. For me, it's cooking something fun (read: time-consuming and messy) and having a movie night with my husband. Step back and recharge, then get your brave on and put yourself out there again.

A Note From Jill on Rejection

One of the first books on craft I read was Stephen King's *On Writing*, and the number of times Stephen had been rejected before he finally published something was probably over a hundred times. In his book he talks about sticking all the rejections on a nail on the wall until the papers were inches thick. But Stephen kept on writing and submitting anyway.

So I got it in my head that I might get rejected at least one hundred times too, and if I wanted this thing bad enough, I was going to have to deal with that. So, when I got my first rejection, I danced. Only ninety-nine to go, I told myself. Whoo hoo!

That philosophy kept me thinking positive about rejections. It gave me the chance to learn to write without putting all my hopes in every envelope I sent out. And, yeah. I was still disappointed when I got rejected. But it helped that I knew not to get my hopes up just yet. It helped to tell myself that I was learning how to do this thing and it might take a while to get it right.

The cool thing? I only received about sixteen rejections before I published my first article.

Step 5
Building a Career

Rinse and Repeat
by Stephanie

My writer friend Roseanna M. White once referred to our industry as a rinse and repeat industry, and the truth of it stuck with me. Because even if you've written a killer manuscript, shined her up beautifully, landed a literary agent and a book contract with your gorgeous book proposal . . . your job's not over.

For one thing, there are more books to write. And there are no shortcuts with that. Well, there are. I think we've all experienced falling in love with a well-known author, and then watching their stories start to all sound the same, or start to flat-out suck. None of us aspire to be like that, right? We want our characters to keep getting deeper, our plots to keep getting twistier, and our themes to hit home stronger.

And you do that by "rinsing and repeating."

I'm multi-published, have had my books translated into another language (Dutch), have an all-star for an agent, have been on the cover of the Kansas City Star, and so forth. Even still, if I want to keep writing books for a living, I have to "rinse and repeat." Here are some ways that I do that:

I attend writers conferences.

Not only do I get a chance to network with other writers and editors, I get to take classes and learn from writers who I admire. About once a conference, I find myself in a class that isn't helpful to me, but the majority of them have at least a nugget I can take home.

I read craft books.

I continue to buy, borrow, and enjoy craft books. I'll say that at this point in my career, it's getting harder for me to be impressed by an entire book, but I often find something new that I want to try with my next project. I also continue to reread my favorites, and at each rereading, I find I understand them differently.

I reach out to other writers.

Often I reach out to others about appearing on the Go Teen Writers blog—at first glance this may not seem like a real rinse and repeat activity, but it is. Because I typically only go to one conference a year, if I want to network with other writers, it has to be done on-line. Sometimes reaching out goes well. Sometimes I never hear back.

I try new genres.

I write quickly simply because I write five days a week and neglect things like email or vacuuming. When I had a handful of completed contemporary YA manuscripts sitting around, plus a few proposals for unfinished contemporary YAs, I asked my agent if she would be okay with me working on a different genre. She encouraged me, and I had a blast writing it. Maybe it'll sell, maybe it won't. But wow, did I have fun. Totally stretched me as a writer.

A word of caution about exploring different genres. As an artist it's annoying to think about having to specify one genre we want to write in for the rest of our lives. Especially for someone who likes writing all kinds of books and has a variety of story ideas. But if you're a career novelist, you have to keep your readers in mind. Not to say you have to write the same kind of book over and over, or that you can never explore other genres or nuances of genres, but you'll need a way to bring your readers with you.

One of my favorite established authors is Sarah Dessen, who writes contemporary YA fiction. I love her books, and she's one of the few authors whose books I pre-order. She writes books about ordinary girls, their summer vacations, and the boys in their lives. Love 'em.

But if Sarah's next book was on, say, violent teenage witches and their battles with the Amish, I would feel, somehow, like her promise to me had been broken. You as a reader have certain expectations about the authors you love, and if they were to veer wildly, it would probably leave you unsettled. Well, your readers will feel the same way. Your name on the cover will eventually make promises to them, and you want to keep those promises because you'll love your readers.

I continue to dig deeper with my ideas.

I used to write in a vacuum. I had no writing friends, and I wasn't a part of any kind of writing organization. So when I had a new idea for a story, I would get super excited about it, share it with my husband in an, "Isn't this the best idea ever???" kind of way, and then set about writing it.

Now when I have a story idea, I still get super excited, but I take a different approach. I invite other trusted writers into the process, typically Jill and Roseanna White. I write a rough blurb and send it to them with questions like, "Have you seen this done before? What if I did such-and-such instead? Do you see any holes in this?" I invite them into the process, and in doing so, I identify and fix plot problems before I write a word.

I communicate with my readers and followers.

Apparently not all writers do this because when I'm sitting in marketing classes one of the things they always advise is to write back to readers and respond to comments on your blog posts.

For me, I'm just so stinkin' excited that people are reading my books and writing to me about them, or that people are hanging out at the blog and joining the conversation, that I can't help but respond. Responding to emails and comments takes up increasingly more of my work time, but I've kept it a priority.

I attend local writing groups and author events.

A lot of the big writing organizations (like Romance Writers of America or Society of Children's Book Writers and Illustrators) have local chapters as well. The writer's organization I'm a member of has a Kansas City chapter that meets once a month. I'm only able to make it a couple times a year, usually, but it's been a really valuable place to socialize with other writers. Also, I attend events for other authors when I can, such as book signings and readings of writers I admire. Not to gain anything (other than an autographed book), just to be out there.

I have kept the same critique partner.

While there are certainly reasons to find new critique partners, either because a relationship is toxic or they can provide different insights into your stories, holding onto a good one is vital. The biggest benefits I see are:

We don't have to balance "fix this" comments with "this is good" comments because we trust each other and feel secure in the relationship.

She knows what I'm capable of, and if something's falling short, she'll push me to do better.

The last thing I want to say about building a career is a stolen slogan from a car company—"The destination is the journey."

If you're doing this thing the right way, I'm of the opinion that you'll never arrive at a destination. You might hit milestones along the way—the New York Times bestseller list or simply an email from a reader who was changed by your book. Even if you become the next Stephen King—whose name seems to be synonymous with the phrase "successful writer"—there's always the next book you want to write.

There's nothing wrong with wanting your writing to be successful and pushing yourself to achieve the next professional step. Just don't forget to enjoy the journey, enjoy the writing, and respect your dream!

Relax, Learn, and Don't Cheat
by Jill

I started out writing with a goal of making a difference with my stories. And the more I realized that I had to learn, I got distracted from my original goal. Getting published became everything. It was my method of proving I was good enough to go back and continue with that goal of making a difference.

My logic was a bit flawed. Anyone can make a difference in the world at any moment. One doesn't need to have a published book to do it. But being published became my obsession, and I didn't stop until I found success. And it wouldn't have been possible without the journey of learning and failure.

Now that I've published several books, things have shifted again. I still write to make a difference with my stories, but now I also want to be successful for my publishers. I'd feel bad if they took a risk on me that flopped. And I also don't want to disappoint my readers. So, I take my writing very seriously. I worry over it. I drive my husband crazy with questions. "Do you think this works okay?" "What do you think of this line?"

One thing that's important to me is to give back. I'm a teacher by nature, and I like to help people. I get so excited that I often forget to ask if the person wants help. But I remember how confused I was in the beginning, and I know it would have been so great just to have an author to ask questions of every once in a while. So I try to give back. I blog. I teach at conferences. I speak at schools. I give away free critiques. I answer questions via email.

I read all the time. I want to know what books are popular in the young adult genre. I read my critique partners' stories. And publishers send me books to read for potential endorsement. Plus I still read books on writing to improve my craft. Reading is a big part of my job. And every once in a while I read a book just for kicks.

I'm always brainstorming new ideas, but because I'm under contract, I can't always work on them. Usually I start a new notebook or file folder, jot down my ideas, then shelve them for later. I have way too many ideas. Just ask my agent.

So before I was published, I spent all my time writing to learn. And now that I'm published I write because I'm contracted to. I'm still always trying to learn, but now it really is a full-time job. I have to be careful to spend my time wisely so I can get those books written. And I have to market myself too, spending time online and speaking and teaching and doing book signings.

Being a career novelist is hard work. My back aches, my arms and shoulders ache. I'll likely need glasses soon. But I wouldn't trade it for any other job. Not even being a fashion designer with her own patternmakers and seamstresses. Not even for being a rock star or an actress. This job is my calling; I have no doubt. And when you're living your life, fulfilling your purpose, it's the best thing ever.

In Closing . . .

We wish we could clean up the road for you.

We wish we could break down those obstacles like the hole in your story that you can't seem to figure out, or the nerves tightening your gut when you pitch to an agent at a conference, or the bite of a rejection from a dream publisher. We wish we could remove those horrible moments like when you spend a year writing and perfecting a story . . . only to find out that an established author *just* released one that's eerily similar.

As much as we wish to, we can't prepare the road for you. But we can prepare *you* for the road.

That's what we strive to do five days a week online at GoTeenWriters.com, and it's why we wrote this book. We know the tenacity it takes to stick with writing, and we know the heartache involved. We know sometimes you'll wish you *could* quit. You'll wish you didn't love writing so much, that writing stories didn't make you feel so complete and purposeful, because you're tired of reworking this story, and you just want to hang up your pen or close down your word processor forever.

We get that.

(Chocolate sometimes helps, by the way.)

But much like the characters that you send out on journeys, you have your own unique quest to go on. You have your own story to live, and writing is part of your story. And what's a good story without conflict, twists, and obstacles?

You want to be a writer. Don't take shortcuts.

Because when you:

•Squelch your pride while you listen to your critique group review your book,

•Go over your manuscript with a red pen *yet again*,

•Scrap that beginning that isn't working and start over,

•Pay for a quality freelance editor instead of a vanity press,

•Save your allowance for a writers conference,

•Send out another batch of queries to literary agents you've

researched,
•Keep on writing despite all the rejections you've received,

That is when you're respecting the journey you're on rather than looking for shortcuts. That's when you're living a good story.
Dare to dream on.

With encouragement,

Stephanie and Jill

Extras:
Lists and Resources

The Go Teen Writers
Self-Editing Checklist

Macro Edit

Plot

Is my story problem established early? Why should the reader care? How is the beginning of my story? Have I:

• Shown the main character in his home world?
• Presented my main character with an invitation to go on a journey?
• Made it so he *chooses* to go on the journey? Have I given him a compelling enough reason?
• Established my character's goal?

How is the middle of my story? Have I:

• Given my main character multiple people, places, activities, or objects to love and fight for?
• Presented my characters with multiple obstacles to overcome?
• Designed several big twists in the story?
• Created a big midpoint scene?
• Created a clear disaster that leads to an "all hope is lost" moment for the character?
• Made my other characters (antagonist and secondary) active? Are they living lives of their own?

How is the end of my story? Have I:

• Locked my main character into a final battle of sorts?
• Written a convincing win or loss?
• Written a denouement that fits the story?

Characters

Does my main character . . .

•Have an internal and external goal? What does he or she want most in the world?
•Have an inner desire? (Love, respect, honor)
•Believe in a lie?
•Choose to go on the story journey? If not, what would have to happen for him to choose to go?
•Have multiple people, places, or objects he loves?
•Go through grief when he loses something?

Does my antagonist . . .

•Have an internal and external goal of his own?
•Actively work to foil the plans of my main character?
•Have a compelling backstory and inner desire?
•Believe in a lie?
•Have anything or anyone he cares about?

Do the other characters in the story . . .

•Have different backstories from each other?
•Have problems of their own?
•Have something they want? Does it conflict with what the main character is trying to achieve?
•Oppose or challenge my main character's worldview?

Setting

Have I taken time to consider my main character's feelings about the setting?

What needs to be researched still?

What are the "laws" for my setting or magic and are they consistent with each other? (Applies mostly to fantasy/sci-fi.)

Theme

Did any themes grow organically when I wrote the story? If so, what are they?

Is there a way I can draw them out further?

Is there a symbol I can use?

Is this a theme my antagonist embraces as well or no?

Micro Edit

Check each scene for use of:

Point of View

Did I do a good job picking my POV character for each scene?

Did I share anything that the POV character wouldn't know?

Do I jump into anyone else's thoughts *or* do I try too hard to broadcast the thoughts and feelings of another character in the scene?

Run a search for the words "they" or "their." Can I replace any of these with words that better reflect my POV character?

How is my balance of inner monologue? Am I letting the reader draw close to the character?

Backstory and Flashbacks

Did I over-explain anything in this scene?

Did I tell the backstory from the POV characters worldview?

If a flashback is used, did I put it at a time that makes sense?

Dialogue

Did I punctuate my dialogue in a way that makes my meanings clear?

Did my characters use different words and phrases from each other?

Have I considered this conversation from the views of all

participants?

Run a search for "said," "asked," and other dialogue tags I use often. Is there an action tag or thought beat that would work better?

Why is my character saying this *now*? Why does she feel this is the right/best time?

Are there places where I info dump in my dialogue? Pay close attention to spots where I refer to time. ("Since today is Thursday, your assignment is due in two days.")

In group conversations, how is the pacing? Is everyone pulling their own weight in the conversation?

Telling and Showing

Run a search for telling words: notice, found, spotted, experienced, looked, feeling, felt, watched, wondered, listened, tried, seemed, and thought. Did I use these words well? Or did I rely on them for telling the story instead of showing it?

Search for telling adverbs. Am I saying "he walked quickly" when I could say "he rushed?"

Run a search for the phrase "with a" and see if I tried to sneak in some telling that way too.

Description

Did I give context for my scenes within the first paragraph (location, characters, time)?

Did I describe things through the eyes of my POV character?

Did I mention any items that may be important later? (If someone throws a vase at the end of the scene, make sure to mention it when describing the room.)

Was I smart about my word choice? Did I pick specific nouns, verbs, and adjectives that help set the mood for my story?

What senses (taste, touch, smell, feel, hear) have I used in each scene? Can I use more or different ones?

Freshening and Tightening Your Writing

Survey the length of sentences. Do I need to vary them?
Can I break up any long paragraphs?
Read the scene for clichés and overused phrases.
Apply the words of George Orwell to every sentence:
1. What am I trying to say?
2. What words will best express it?
3. Is there an image or idiom that will make it clear?
4. Is this image fresh enough to have an effect?

Run a search for the word "it" and see if I can use a more specific word, especially if it's the start of a sentence.

Are there places I used two words when I could use one instead?

Have I chosen the best possible words? Active, concrete words?

Search for the words: as, when, while, after, and continued to. Make sure those sentences are in a logical order—action, then reaction.

Hunt down passive phrases—search each scene for "was" or "is" depending on the tense of the book.

Check any sentences that begin with —ing words.

Check any sentences that use the phrases "began to" or "started to."

Have I formatted everything correctly?

Is my title page single spaced and my manuscript double spaced?

Am I using 12-point Times New Roman or Courier font?

Does each chapter begin on a new page?

Do I have one space after punctuation, not two?

Run Spell Check

Double-check for correct punctuation, grammar, and common typos:

Run a search for those tricky words and any others I tend to misspell:
"Chance" when I meant "change"
Its/it's
Know/now
Loose/lose
Past/passed
They're/their/there
Thing/think
Though/through/thought

Run a search for my placeholders.

What's a placeholder?

Many writers, when they come across something they need to research or write in more detail but don't want to take the time right then, they'll put in a placeholder word or symbol to mark that they need to come back.

Stephanie uses the word "GIRAFFE" for things she needs to fill in or an asterisk (*) if she's not happy with a phrase but doesn't have the brainpower at the moment to fix it. Jill tends to highlight the place that needs a little more love, or she'll add a comment to remind herself what she needs to come back and finish.

While typically you'll have fixed them all by the end of the micro edit, always run a check for your placeholders just to be sure!

Self-Editing Dialogue Checklist

A writer on the Go Teen Writers blog asked if we could make one of these. Hopefully you find it helpful as well!

___ Are you trusting your dialogue and using action beats, or are you trying to make up for weak dialogue with lots of, "she retorted" and "he exclaimed" and she "expostulated"?

___ Are your characters strategic about what they say, or are they just blurting things out? Did they enter the conversation with a plan?

___ When your characters receive tough news or bad breaks, are they processing the situation and experiencing grief in a realistic way?

___ Have you fallen into a "Q & A" pattern anywhere? Where one character is doing nothing but asking questions and the other character is doing nothing but answering them?

___ Do your characters use different words for the same thing, or are their phrasings too similar? (Grocery store can also be the market, purses can also be handbags.)

___ Are you letting character/story information come out naturally, or are you trying to explain too much with your dialogue? ("Gee, Bob, I'm so glad it's our anniversary today and that we've been married for seven years and have two beautiful children!")

___ Does every character behave and interact as though they believe *they* are the main character?

___ Are you using contractions?

___ Is your dialogue age-appropriate? Or are your toddlers elegant and your grannies saying words like "peeps" for anything other than marshmallow chicks. (*Shudder.* Don't know why, but I *hate* the word peeps.)

___ Do you have too many "group" conversations? (Conversations with four or more.)

___ Is "small talk" bogging down your story? (Hi, how are you? Good, how are you? Good. Nice day we're having. Sure is. And so on.)

___ Do you have a good balance of internal thoughts and dialogue? Does the reader get a sense of not only what the point-of-view character is saying, but *why* he's saying it and what he *feels* about the conversation in general?

___ Have you considered conversations from the perspective of all the characters involved, not just the point-of-view character?

Stephanie & Jill's
Weasel Words & Phrases

These are words we overuse or that sneak into our first drafts despite our best efforts to keep them out.

Stephanie's

Quirked (my characters are always quirking eyebrows)
So-and-so rolled her eyes/ran her hands through her hair
Like
Just
Were
Was
Said
Asked
Very
Smile(d)
Sigh(ed)
Really
"Or something" (I like to throw that in to the end of a lot of my sentences for some reason. "We should go to the movies or something.")
Past/Passed—I have issues remembering which is correct.
It—Especially at the start of sentences. Often "it" should be replaced with something more specific.

Jill's

Vague words

Many, few, lots, a lot of, a little, some, most, almost, more, a few, rather, might, perhaps, much, often, for the most part, like, seem, etc.

Absolutes

Every, very, entire, everyone, everything, etc.

Verbs that facilitate telling

Feel/felt, see/saw, hear/heard, think/thought, look, watch, taste, smell, wonder, decide, notice, remember, recall, consider, ponder, is, am, are, was, were, has, had, have, etc.

Infinite Verb Phrases (Starting sentences with —ing words)

Continuous action words

As, when, while, after, continued to.

Pronouns

Overuse of "they" or "them" tends to create the feel of an omniscient POV.

Time transitions

Just, then, as, the next day, all at once, soon, etc.

Adverbs

Softly, angrily, sadly, really, basically, immediately, very, actually, surely, usually, truly, suddenly, etc.

Double verbs

Started to, began to.

Some other words on my list

Thought/though/through, loose/lose, there, it, be, being, been, became, that, well, poor, anyway, quite, however, about.

Story Brainstorming Questions

When you have a new story idea, these questions are meant to help you take it deeper.

Character Questions (for major characters)

Who is my character?
What is she named and why?
If I had to describe her in one word, it would be:
What's her family like?
What does she value?
What lie does she believe?
Why does she believe that lie? What happened in her past that caused her to believe it?
What is her main goal in the story?
Why is she ideal for the journey and why is she not?
Who are her allies and who are her enemies?
What will my main character sacrifice?
How does she need to change?
What happens if she doesn't meet her goals? Why are her goals important? How can I make that worse for her? Who else could it impact?
In what ways is she operating against society and in what ways is she operating within?
What part of her past can come back to haunt her?
What is her greatest fear?

Other Character Questions

What does the antagonist want?
Does my antagonist have a secret he's trying to keep?
Who will make sacrifices for my main character throughout the story?
What character could come out of the shadows and "shine?"

Go Teen Writers - Stephanie Morrill & Jill Williamson

Story Questions

What's the best place for the story to start?

How do I think it will end? What is the climax?

Does my story have a theme? Why does this book matter?

What kind of hurdles will there be in the journey? How can I make these harder? How can I make them "cost" my main character more?

What is my storyworld like? Are there political, historical, or environmental situations that might affect my character's journey?

Is there magic in my story? If so, how does it work? What are the rules, costs, and limitations for it?

Story Plotting Charts

These can help in the early stages of planning your book or when editing to help you see what's missing. Download the full-sized documents at: www.jillwilliamson.com/teenage-authors/helps/

Scene Plotting Chart

STORY TITLE: _____
Beginning:
Inciting Incident:
Second Thoughts:
Climax of act 1:
Obstacle:
Obstacle:
Midpoint twist:
Obstacle:
Disaster:
Crisis:
Climax of act 2:
Climax of act 3:
Obstacles:
Denouement:
End:

Scene Plotting Chart for Two Points of View

_____'s POINT OF VIEW	_____'s POINT OF VIEW
Beginning: Inciting Incident:	Beginning: Inciting Incident:
Second Thoughts: Climax of act 1:	Second Thoughts: Climax of act 1:
Obstacle:	Obstacle:
Obstacle:	Obstacle:
Midpoint twist:	Midpoint twist:
Obstacle:	Obstacle:
Disaster:	Disaster:
Crisis:	Crisis:
Climax of act 2:	Climax of act 2:
Climax of act 3:	Climax of act 3:
Obstacles:	Obstacles:
Denouement:	Denouement:
End:	End:

Character Archetypes

This is a fun list that can help you with brainstorming your characters.

Analyst: Can explain anything rationally. Ex: Mr. Spock

Anti-hero: The hero who didn't ask to get involved but does. Ex: Sarah Connor, Wolverine

Benefactor: Has a whole lot of something he wants to share. Ex: Miss Havisham

Bully: Has no tolerance for weakness, especially in himself. Ex: Scut Farkus (*Christmas Story*)

Bureaucrat: Follows the rules no matter what. Ex: Hermione Granger

Caretaker: Cares for others. Ex: Digory Kirke

Catalyst: Makes things happen.

Child: Could be a literal child or just living like one. Ex: Wally McDoogle, Peter Pan

Coward: Afraid of everything, controlled by fear. Ex: Adrian Monk, Cowardly Lion, Alexandra Rover

Curmudgeon: Irritable and cynical and proud of it. Ex: Ebenezer Scrooge

Dreamer: Longs to be something else. Ex: Annie, William Thatcher (*A Knight's Tale*)

Elder/mentor/teacher/parent: Been around long enough to know some vital information. Ex: Ben Kenobi, Mufassa

Explorer/wanderer: Wants to see the world—could be running from something.

Extraordinary man: The guy who can do anything. Ex: Indiana Jones, James Bond

Gossip: Must be the first to know everything and the one to pass it on. Ex: Rachel Lynde

Guardian: Protects the weak.

Hedonist/thrill-seeker: Lives for today in case tomorrow never comes.

Herald/messenger: The bringer of news, good, bad, or necessary.

Hermit/loner: Just wants to be left alone. Ex: Phil Hercules, Martin Riggs (*Lethal Weapon*)

Hunter/predator: Can catch or kill anything. Ex: Terminator

Innocent: An inexperienced individual exposed to the evils in the world. Ex: Dorothy Gale

Introvert: Lives inside his shell to prevent anyone from seeing the real him. Ex: Gabriella Montez (*High School Musical*)

Investigator: Thrives on puzzles and riddles. Ex: Nancy Drew, Sherlock Holmes

Judge/mediator: The arbitrator or peacemaker in a conflict.

Leader: Always knows the best thing to do—and the people follow him. Ex: William Wallace

Magician/wizard/superhero: Has special powers or abilities. Ex: Superman, Harry Potter

Manipulator: Plays with people and situations to get what he wants. Ex: Scarlett O'Hara

Martyr: Willing to suffer or die for others or a cause.

Masochist: Finds pleasure in torturing himself, denying himself—may take on too much.

Masquerader: Pretends to be something he's not.

Monster: A depraved beast. Ex: Gollum, Grendel (*Beowulf*)

Ordinary man: Your average Joe, just like you or me or the guy across the street. Ex: Dr. Richard Kimball, Frodo Baggins.

Penitent: Lives to atone for his sin.

Perfectionist: Every action and word must be flawless.

Pleaser/show-off: Craves approval from anyone and may do anything to get it.

Poet: Life is art, be that through story, song, painting, or sculpture.

Rebel/revolutionary: Stands opposed to the status quo and fights for his cause.

Rogue: Looks out for himself and no one else. Ex: Han Solo

Saboteur/betrayer: For whatever reason, he will make sure something fails. Ex: Edmund Pevensie

Samaritan: Does good deeds wherever he goes.

Scholar: Wants to learn.

Sensualist: Addicted to feeling good about himself.

Slave: Does not belong to himself. Ex: Dobby the house elf
Survivor: Pulls through no matter what happens, doesn't give up.
Sycophant: Self-seeking, flatterer, who works to please those in power. Ex: Smee (*Peter Pan*)
Temptress: Uses power (intellect, magic, beauty) to make others weak. Ex: Megara (*Hercules*)
Thief: Takes what he wants or needs. Ex: Philippe Gaston (*LadyHawke*), Jean Valjean
Trickster/jester: Always looking for the humor in a situation. Ex: Fred and George Weasley
Tyrant: Must be in control at all times. Ex: Captain Hook
Victim: Was hurt by someone or lives in fear that someone will hurt him. Ex: Claireece "Precious" Jones
Villain: Seeks to destroy/trap the hero. Ex: Evil Queen in *Snow White*, Lex Luthor
Waif: Appears innocent and weak and often relies on the pity of others. Ex: The Kid (*Dick Tracy*)

Hobbies & Skills Brainstorming List

Are all your characters writers or artists or soccer players? Here's a list that can help you shake things up.

Art and Crafts

Airbrushing	Fly tying (for fly fishing)	Photography
Beading	Glass blowing	Pottery
Blacksmithing	Graphic design	Quilting
Bridge building	Jewelry making	Scrapbooking
Calligraphy	Knitting	Sculpture
Candle making	Leather crafting	Sewing
Cartoons	Macramé	Soap making
Carving	Map making	Stained glass
Crochet	Model cars	Taxidermy
Cross-stich	Model rockets	Tie dying
Dollhouses	Model ships	Weaving
Drawing	Needlepoint	Woodworking
Embroidery	Origami	
Engraving	Painting	

Collecting

Action figures	Collector cards	Petals
Antiques	Comic books	Postcards
Artwork	Diecast	Posters
Barbies	Dolls	Rocks
Books	Guns	Seashells
Buttons	Insects	Sports cards
Cars	Leaves	Stamps
Clothing	Memorabilia	Toys
Coins	Music	

Exercise

Aerobics	Spinning	Yoga
Cardio kickboxing	Sports (see sports list)	Zumba
Pilates	Weight training	

Food

Baking	Canning
Cake decorating	Cooking

Games

Air hockey	Chess	Lawn darts
Backgammon	Crossword puzzles	Online gaming
Billiards	Darts	Paintball
Board games	Dominoes	Poker
Bridge	Dungeons and Dragons	Video games
Cards	Jigsaw puzzles	

Hobbies

Arcade games	Foreign languages	Reading
Astrology	Gambling	Reenactment:
Being a fan of . . .	Garage saleing	Medieval/Civil War
Body art	Genealogy	Remote control toys
Book reviewing	Geocaching	Robotics
Computers	Ham radios	Shopping
Construction	Journaling	Traveling
Domino set ups	Juggling	Trekkie (Star Trek Fan)
Educational courses	Knotting	Watching movies
Electronics	Legos	Watching sports
Fantasy Football	Magician	Watching TV
Fast cars	Modeling	Websites
Film making	Piloting an airplane	Yoyo
Fixing cars	Pinball machines	

Outdoors

Air sports	Fishing	Motorbikes
Archery	Flower competitions	Mountain climbing
Astronomy	Frisbee	Rafting
ATV riding	Gardening	Rock climbing
Beachcombing	Geology	Rodeo
Bicycling	Go-kart racing	Sailing
Bird watching	Gold panning	Scuba diving
Board sports	Hang gliding	Shooting guns
Boating	Hiking	Skateboarding
Bonsai trees	Horseback riding	Sky diving
Boomerangs	Hot air ballooning	Snorkeling
Building sandcastles	Hunting	Sunbathing
Butterfly watching	Kayaking	Surfing
Camping	Kite boarding	Treasure hunting
Canoeing	Kites	Water sports
Cave diving	Metal detecting	White water rafting
Dumpster diving	Motor sports	Windsurfing

Performance

A cappella singing	Cosplay	Radio
Acting	Dancing	Rock band
Baton twirling	Karaoke	Show choir
Beatboxing	Marching band	Singing
Bell choir	Orchestra/band	Theater sports
Choir	Playing an instrument	Worship team
Church choir	Podcasting	Youth band
Comedy	Puppetry	

261

Pets

Bee keeping	Fish	Pigs
Bird	Guinea pig	Snake
Cat	Hamster	Spider
Cows	Horses	Turtle
Dog	Lambs	
Falconry	Lizard	

Service

Big brother/sister	Reading to kids
Candy striper	Rescuing animals
Children's church	Retirement home volunteer
Food collection	Rocking sick babies
Habitat for Humanity	Tutoring
Lunch buddy	Volunteering
Reading to elderly	Youth group

Social

Bars	Dating
Chatting	Entertaining
Clubbing	Skype
Dancing	Texting
Dining out	

Writing

Blogging	Music- songs
Fan fiction	Newspaper
Fiction- novels	Playwright
Fiction- short stories	Poetry
Magazines	Scriptwriting
Music- composition	

Sports

Badminton	Field events	Running
Baseball	Figure skating	Snowboarding
Basketball	Football	Soccer
BMX tricks	Golf	Softball
Bowling	Gymnastics	Street racing
Car racing	Ice hockey	Swimming
Cheerleading	Martial arts	Tennis
Cricket	Parkour	Volleyball
Cross country skiing	Polo	Water polo
Diving	Racing bicycles	Wrestling
Downhill skiing	Racquetball	
Fencing	Rugby	

Character Traits Brainstorming List

For kicks, try closing your eyes and circling a few random ones!

active	cold-hearted	doesn't learn
adventurous	compassionate	domineering
affectionate	competitive	doubtful
afraid	complacent	dutiful
aggressive	compulsive	eager
ambitious	conceited	easygoing
amiable	confident	eloquent
angry	confused	encouraging
animated	considerate	energetic
annoyed	cooperative	enthusiastic
anti-social	courageous	fair
anxious	cowardly	faithful
argumentative	crafty	fearless
arrogant	critical	fidgety
attentive	cruel	fierce
babyish	cultured	finicky
blabbermouth	curious	foolish
bored	cynical	formal
bossy	dangerous	frank
brave	daring	friendly
brilliant	decisive	frustrated
busy	dependable	funny
calm	dependent	generous
careful	determined	gentle
cautious	diligent	giddy
charismatic	discreet	giving
charming	dishonest	glamorous
cheerful	disloyal	gloomy
childish	disobedient	grateful
clever	disparaging	greedy
clumsy	disrespectful	grouchy
coarse	dissatisfied	gullible

265

happy	insolent	noisy
harried	intelligent	obedient
hateful	jealous	obliging
haughty	judgmental	obnoxious
helpful	lackadaisical	observant
honest	languid	obsessive
hopeful	lazy	overindulgent
hopeless	liar	prejudice
hospitable	logical	procrastinator
humble	lonely	reckless
hyper	loving	rude
ignorant	loyal	sarcastic
ill-bred	lucky	selfish
imaginative	malicious	self-pitying
immature	mature	shy
impartial	mean	smart
impatient	meticulous	stubborn
impolite	mischievous	superficial
impudent	moody	tactless
impulsive	mundane	takes self too seriously
inappropriate	mysterious	too trusting
inconsiderate	naive	unable to commit
independent	negligent	uncommunicative
industrious	nervous	unconfident
innocent	never satisfied	unmannered
insensitive	no sense of humor	untrusting

Character Phobias Brainstorming List

abandoned	dreams/nightmares
airplanes, birds overhead	drowning/water
beards (facial hair)	dust
bees	elderly
being alone	elevators
being embarrassed	enclosed spaces
being looked at	endings
being poor	everything
being tortured	failure
being touched	falling
big crowds	fear
birds	feet
blood	fire
bridges	fish
bombs	flying
cats	food someone else made
cell phones	forests
cemeteries	frogs
changes	frying pans
children	germs
clocks	getting arrested
closets	getting fat
clowns	ghosts
colors (a certain one)	going to sleep (never waking)
commitment	guns/weapons
conspiracies	heights
crossing roads	hospitals
dark	household appliances
death of a loved one	intimacy
death of self	ladders
dirt	leadership
disappointing someone	losing things (therefore hoards)
dogs	making decisions
dolls	meat

267

medication	saying goodbye
men or women	scary movies
messes (or any untidiness)	seafood
mirrors	shadows
monsters	sharks
moths	sickness
needles or pointed objects	snakes
noises	speaking in public
nudity	spiders
numbers (a certain one)	stairs
oceans/lakes	staying single
old age (getting old)	strangers
open closets/doors	sunlight
outside	thunder and lightning
pain	traffic
police officers	trapped/small spaces/buried alive
raw food	turning out like parent
rejection	war
relationships	weather (storms)
riding in vehicles	worms
rollercoasters	x-rays

Historical Periods

Unsure about what historical genre your book falls in? This list can help. And this list only covers Europe and North America. You can also research historical periods for other parts of the world.

The Stone Age - The Beginning to 2000 BC
The Bronze Age - 3600 BC–600 BC
The Iron Age - 1200BC–400AD
Barbarian Invasions - 300AD–700AD
Medieval - 400AD–1500AD
Renaissance - 1500AD–1700AD
Elizabethan (UK) - 1558AD–1603AD
Jacobean (UK) - 1603AD–1625AD
Caroline (UK) - 1625–1649
Interregnum (UK) - 1649–1660
Restoration (UK) - 1660–1688
Georgian (UK) - 1714–1830
Napoleonic Era (FR) - 1799–1815
Regency (UK) - 1811–1837
Victorian (UK) - 1837–1901
Edwardian (UK) - 1901–1910
Colonial - 1492–1775
Native American - 1492–1900
Revolution - 1775–1800
Turn of the 19th Century - 1795–1810
West - 1800–1890
Regency era in Europe/Federal era in the US - 1811–1820
War of 1812 - 1812
Antebellum - 1820–1861
Victorian UK/US - 1837–1901
Frontier - 1845–1916
South - 1860–1920
Civil War - 1861–1865
Reconstruction - 1865–1887
Turn of the Century - 1890–1915

World War I - 1914–1918
Interwar period - 1918–1939
Roaring Twenties - 1920–1929
Great Depression - 1929–World War II
World War II - 1939–1945
Post WWII - 1945–1950
Atomic Age - after 1945
Post-war era - 1946–1962
Cold War (Soviet Union and US) -1945–1989 or 1991
Space Age - after 1957
The Sixties - 1960–1969
Turbulent 1960's/War in Vietnam
Post-Modern (Soviet Union and United States) -1973–present
Information Age - 1970–present
The Seventies - 1970–1979
The Eighties - 1980–1989
The Nineties - 1990–1999
The 2000s - 2000–2009
The Social Age - 2004–present
The Tens - 2010–2019
The Big Data age - 2001–present

Glossary of Terms

Abbreviations

ABA: American Booksellers Association
ARC: Advance reading copy
BCC: Back cover copy
BEA: BookExpo America
CBA: Christian Booksellers Association
FMC: Female main character
GTW: Go Teen Writers
ISBN: International Standard Book Number
K: Thousand, as in an 80,000-word novel or 80K novel
MC: Main character
MMC: Male main character
MS: Manuscript *or* Microsoft (as in MS Word)
NaNoWriMo: National Novel Writing Month
OP: Out of print
POV: Point of view
SASE: Self-addressed stamped envelope
SCBWI: Society of Children's Book Writers and Illustrators
WC: Word count
WIP: Work in progress

Publishing Industry Terms

Acquisitions editor: A publishing house employee who reads incoming manuscripts to seek out publishable material.

Advance: A sum of money paid to the author in anticipation of royalty earnings, often pain in increments.

Agent: A person that represents an author's work and tries to sell it to editors.

Content editor (also known as a developmental or substantive editor): A person who edits a book for overall plot issues, character development, and continuity of the story.

Cover letter: A letter sent with a manuscript or proposal to introduce the author and his project to an editor or agent.

Fiction: Works of the imagination, made-up stories.

Independent (Indie) publisher: A small publisher. Some pay an advance, some don't. Many are too small to get into bookstores, though some can.

Line editor: A person who goes over every sentence in a manuscript to make sure there are no errors.

Manuscript: A typed out story, article, or novel.

National Novel Writing Month: An organization that encourages participants to write at least 50,000 words in one month.

Nonfiction: Works that are not fictional.

Proofreader: A person who reads a final manuscript for errors.

Proposal: A thorough presentation of an author's book to an editor or agent for publication.

Query letter: A letter an author writes to propose his project to an editor or agent. Usually one page long.

Self-addressed stamped envelope (SASE): An envelope that an author addresses to himself with sufficient postage that he sends along with his query letter or manuscript so that the editor or agent can mail the decision back to the author.

Self-publishing: And author pays to have his ebook or paperback book published.

Slush pile: The imaginary and sometimes literal "pile" of manuscripts that have been sent to an agent or editor without an invitation. (You don't want your manuscript here.)

Synopsis: A one to two page summary of the plot of a novel.

Traditional publishing: This is the standard way an author gets a book published that should get his books into bookstores. In this type of publishing, the publisher pays the author for his book.

Unsolicited: When an author sends in her work to an editor or agent without permission to do so.

Writing Craft Terms

Action tag: Action used to identify the speaker of words spoken in quotes. Ex: "Fine!" Sherry slammed the door.

Backdrop: The setting of your story.

Backstory: What happened to your characters before your story began.

Conflict: That which causes your character to struggle.

Flashback: Inserting an earlier event into the chronological structure of a story.

Narrative: When the story moves into narration, or telling, to explain what's happening outside a character point of view.

Point of view (POV): The position of the narrator who's telling the story at that moment.

Said tag: Used to identify the speaker of words spoken in quotes. Ex: "Do what you want," Sherry said.

Scene: A section of a story that represents a single episode or event.

Our Writing Schedules

Stephanie's Current Work Time Breakdown

With little kids in the house, I manage about fifteen hours a week of work time, plus I do an hour or so in the evenings after the kiddos are in bed. My daily work time breaks down into four main categories:

Current Project: 7½ hours per week

This is, as you might guess, whatever project is going on right then. It might be:
Writing or editing a novel. (This is the most common one.)
Marketing a new release.
Curriculum for a class I'm about to teach.

Go Teen Writers: 4½ hours per week

The time I designate for the blog includes writing the posts, responding to comments, putting together the newsletter, interacting on the Facebook group, or lining up guests.

Interactions: 2 hours per week

I schedule myself a set amount of time for email as well as interacting on Facebook and Twitter. Otherwise social media and email devour my work time.

Administrative: 1 hour per week

I use this time for things an admin would do for me if I had one. Mailing books to readers, determining winners of contests, website maintenance, that kind of stuff. Unless I'm in a marketing season, I also use this time for author interviews.

Jill's Nine-to-Five, Err, Six-to-Four

Every night, I try to make a To Do list for the next day. I have a massive To Do folder with things that have been in there for over a year. I go through the folder and decide what's urgent and what can wait.

I get up around 6:00 am every day. This is not my fault. I live with a few early birds.

I try to start each day reading my Bible, but I often forget. The days I read are always much better days that the days I skip it.

I try to spend about fifteen minutes on email and another fifteen minutes on social media before tackling my To Do list.

I do a few quick things on the list like emails or interviews, then I start writing. I write until my husband comes home for lunch.

After lunch I might continue writing, especially if I'm on a deadline, or I might work on another project from my To Do list, maybe marketing related.

Some other types of things that are often on my To Do list are:

•Update my websites
•Manage contests on my websites
•Fill out blog interviews
•Follow-up with book reviewers
•Answer emails from readers and other writers
•Critique things for my critique partners
•Design ads and such for my website using Photoshop

Monday is my blogging day. I try to write as many posts as I can on that day to leave the rest of the week free for writing.

Tuesdays and Thursdays I do kickboxing class with my husband. This is often the only time I work out each week, so I make myself go. It's also a great brainstorming time.

I try to stop working when I hear the bus pull up and drop off my kids.

Notice how much I've used the word "try" in this list. Life happens . . . I do my best.

Books We Recommend

Self-Editing for Fiction Writers by Renni Browne and Dave King
Revisions and Self-Editing by James Scott Bell
Writing Fiction for Dummies by Randy Ingermanson and Peter Economy
On Writing by Stephen King
Stein on Writing by Sol Stein
Bird by Bird by Anne Lamott
Writing the Breakout Novel and *Writing the Breakout Novel Workbook* by Donald Maass
The Career Novelist by Donald Maass
The Art of War for Writers by James Scott Bell
The Art and Craft of Writing Christian Fiction by Jeff Gerke
Save the Cat by Blake Snyder (A book on screenwriting that will teach you a lot about how to tell a story.)

And for grammar and punctuation, we recommend:
The Chicago Manual of Style
The Elements of Style by Strunk and White

Questions You've Asked

How did/do you juggle everyday life and writing without going insane?

—Katelyn

Stephanie: I'm on the brink of insanity fairly often, and usually it takes my husband speaking sense to me to pull me back to rational thinking. Here are a couple things that have helped me that will hopefully help someone else out there:

1. I draw boundaries around my writing time. With two little ones at home, I get so little focused writing time that I had to draw very clear boundaries around it. I don't answer the phone. I don't respond to instant messages on the computer or text messages. Sometimes this is inconvenient for people in my life who would really like to know *right now* if they can write a guest post on Go Teen Writers or if I can take a meal to a family in a couple weeks. I've taught myself to be comfortable with letting people wait for a couple hours in non-emergency situations. This also means that I don't schedule play dates or lunches with friends during writing time. When my kids are older and not quite so needy, then I'll likely smudge that boundary line from time-to-time, but if I said yes to everything, I would never write.

2. I use my most productive time for writing. There are so many pulls on our time. I identify the time of day that I'm the most productive (pre-kids it was the early morning, now it's their nap times) and use it for writing or writing-related projects, like marketing if I have a release out. I don't move laundry around or send personal emails—I write.

3. I dedicate time to the important people in my life—sometimes by force. Even though it sometimes bugs me when my kids wake up from naps and I'm in the middle of a scene, I'm doing better at remembering how valuable that is. They keep me engaged in the real world, which makes me a healthier, more tuned-in writer. I've also put a few checks and balances in my life—I never work on Sundays, and my husband and I pick a date night every week. We don't always go out, but we do put aside work for the evening in favor of a movie or board game.

Jill: I do go insane. Ask my husband. *wink* But I try to make good choices, to prioritize my family, and to only write when I've set aside time to work.

How do you hold the varied hats of an employee, author, friend, etc?

—Meghan

Stephanie: For me the key has been prioritizing and scheduling, which is often easier said than done. Like I mentioned in my answer about not going insane, I draw very definite boundaries around my writing time. Internally that means I've decided for that hour or thirty minutes or whatever it is, my priority in that moment is writing. It's *not* catching up with a friend from elementary school, mopping my floor, or blogging. The only reason I'm able to do this, though, is because I have time built into my schedule for those things later. Meaning I've scheduled myself time to chat on the phone that evening (possibly *while* I mop my floor) and I know that when my hour of writing is done, I'll get on the blog and respond to comments. Clarifying my priorities to myself and applying them to my calendar has helped me to reduce stress and focus on the task at hand.

One other thing is that we live in a world where we're extremely accessible. If someone wants something from me, they can text me, shoot me an email, send me a chat, or message me on Facebook. All at once, if they like. I've had to train myself to not respond to things right away just because I can or because someone might expect me to. If I tried to respond to everyone who pulled at my attention, I would never get anything done.

Do you have any practical solutions to shutting up the critical voice of "you're not good at this" "you're wasting your time"?

—Tonya

Jill: It helps me to remember that I don't have to please everyone. That makes things a lot less daunting. And while there will always be readers out there who will hate what I write, there are plenty of readers who love it. And they are who I'm writing for. And I'm *not* wasting my time where they're concerned.

It also helps to remember that I chose this. I wanted it bad enough to make it my career. To learn and practice and redo things until I do the best job I can. So even though I go through times where I'm overly stressed and just know I'm going to fail, I remember that I'm not going to give up, so there's no point listening to the voice that's trying to talk me into quitting. I'm in this for the long haul.

Stephanie: I don't have a simple three steps to overcoming this or anything. The only thing that helped me, honestly, was time and getting used to it. I got used to being rejected or critiqued, and it stopped stinging quite so badly.

Because I write bare bones first drafts, I already know that the story is bad . . . and in a weird way, I think that helps me overcome the feeling that what I'm writing isn't good. I already know it isn't good. So when I hear the critical voice, I can just say, "Yeah, I know. We'll fix it after I type the end, okay?"

I have attempted to write a novel numerous times but each time I always lose confidence in myself and give up. I always get paranoid that my stories are boring or that the reader won't like them. Do you have any advice to help me?

—Abi

Jill: Being a writer is hard work. You have to learn to discipline yourself and finish that first draft. It's okay if the story gets a bit boring. You can fix that later. Just keep on writing. You can't fix something that doesn't exist. I try not to worry whether my book is good when I'm writing my first draft. I just write it as fast as I can. Which is why I'm a big fan of National Novel Writing Month. (Check out http://www.nanowrimo.org/ for more information.)

If you get stuck, you might need to add conflict. Conflict is anything that thwarts your main character's goal, and you want to make sure the main character can't achieve his goal until the end of the story. This keeps the reader turning the pages.

Were there ever moments where you just felt like giving up? How did you overcome them?

—Bruno

Stephanie: Yes—all the time! Even now, to be honest. When you get slammed with a vicious review or when a project keeps going to the pub board but not quite passing, it's easy to feel discouraged. More and more I come back to the truth that I love writing and that there's nothing else I would want to do career-wise. When the world of business and publishing has me down, I've found escaping to my story for a full day or week can help me fix my perspective.

When and how did you decide to make the first step into writing an actual novel?

—Arlette

Stephanie: I don't think I ever really decided. I just loved writing, and novels were what naturally came out of my pen. Though they were short and lousy novels.

Jill: When I first started writing, my goal was to write a novel. I was totally naïve, but I stuck with it. I did write articles and short stories later, but the book was my first goal.

How was your writing affected when you had kids? Did you lay it aside for a while or just keep going?
—Ellyn

Stephanie: I was fortunate enough to have a husband who believed in me. When we were first married, and I had a tough time finding part-time work in our college town, he encouraged me to use the time to invest in writing—he didn't have to say it twice! I had about three years of writing full time with no kids, no house to care for, and no real job (I worked a few weeks a year for an event-planning company, but that involved travelling to Puerto Rico, San Diego, and Hawaii, so that hardly counts as work). My intention was to pursue publication until we had kids, pause publication-seeking (but not writing since writing = sanity for me) until the kids were in school, and then resume.

Well, I was holding my one-week-old baby when an agent whom I'd queried months prior asked to see more from me. And when McKenna was four months old, the agent asked to represent me and my YA novel, which became the first book in the Skylar Hoyt series. My daughter was six months old when I signed the contract with Revell. She was eighteen months old when *Me, Just Different* released, two when *Out with the In Crowd* released, and then at my book signing for *So Over It* she was two-and-a-half and Connor was eleven days old.

So it didn't exactly go as planned.

It was a very stressful time—I had acquired a baby, a publishing contract, and a rather large home all within a few months of each other. But they were all good things, and I was determined to make it work. We're fortunate to live in town with my parents and my husband's parents, and they all have flexible work schedules. So we worked out a system where one morning a week my parents watched my daughter (and eventually both kids when Connor came along) and then another morning of the week my in-laws watch them. And combining those mornings with their nap times is really all the work time I want right now. I mean, yeah, I miss the days where I had all day every day to write. But as important as writing is to me, being present in my kids' lives is even more important.

Did you finish the first book you attempted to write?

—Tori

Stephanie: Oh gosh, no. I have tons and tons of books that I started in middle school that never went anywhere. But I learned from each and every one of them. No writing goes to waste!

Jill: Yes! But it wasn't the first book that I had published. My sixth novel was *By Darkness Hid*, the first one that was published. *The New Recruit*, the first book I ever wrote, did eventually get published, but it was my fifth published book.

How do you know when you've found your voice?

—Kylie

Stephanie: I didn't know until an agent said to me, "Wow, you have such a great, fresh voice!" Oh . . . I do? For me, I think, it took writing a main character who was completely different than me. (Skylar from the Skylar Hoyt books.) What started out as a fun experiment, to write a character who thought about life completely different than I did, turned into the catalyst for my voice and publishing career.

Jill: I still don't know if I have an author voice. I know when I've found each character's voice. And I know because it's suddenly so easy to know exactly what he or she will say or do. But my author voice . . . still wondering. Sometimes I think my "author voice" is how I create storyworlds. That seems to be something I do uniquely well.

How long does it typically take to get published?
—Giselle

Stephanie: I don't know if there is a typical, really. Except for "a while." It takes a while to get published. Even people who get published relatively young like I did (I was twenty-four when I signed my contract) have been at it for a long time. I had been writing ever since elementary school and pursuing publication since I was a junior in high school.

How can teens look for an agent and still be taken seriously?
—Renata

Stephanie: I think the market has really opened up to teen writers, so I don't think it's an issue like it might have been in the past. Firstly, you have to be an excellent writer and have a great story to tell. Secondly, professionalism is key. (See Chapter 18.)

Jill: Also, it doesn't hurt to seek out and befriend a published author. There are usually one or two authors at a writers conference who love hanging out with teens. And that author can introduce you to editors and agents if he or she wants to. Don't force it if the author isn't offering, but I've introduced several teen writers to my agent and my editors at writers conferences. But you don't need an author's help, really. You can do it on your own!

Do I need to state that I'm underage in my query letter to an agent or editor? And can teens sign a contract? Do teens get the same rights as adults?
—Marie

Jill: Unless your age is central to the book idea (ex: How I Raised My Triplet Siblings), there's no reason to share your age in a query or cover letter. Write your query letter solely based on your story idea. Make it strong for that reason alone. If you're going to be published as a teen, your writing needs to be as good as those being published as adults. We're all competing for the same publishing slots, you know.

If you're invited to submit more of your book, do so. And only when you're offered a contract do you need to tell them your age. There's no reason a teen author should receive a different offer because he's underage. It's always wise to have an agent look over your contract before you sign it. Contracts are super confusing and you don't want to give away the rights of your book forever. Be careful. And if you're a minor, a parent or guardian might need to sign the contract as well. That might depend on the state you live in.

Now, if you're at a writers conference and meet an editor or agent face to face, you can't hide your age. So play it up. Use it as a marketing strategy. Be bold and personable. Say, "My age is a major asset to any publisher. I live at home, so I have the free time to promote my book. I'm excited to visit schools and talk to students about being published as a teen. Readers will relate to my journey." Things like that. If you're confident and your writing is great, no one will care how old you are.

Do I need to register my manuscript for a copyright before sending it out? Or can I just put a copyright symbol on every page?

—**Ricky**

Jill: There's no reason to put a copyright symbol on anything. The moment you create an original piece of work, copyright laws automatically protect you. Putting a copyright logo on your manuscript marks you as an amateur and sends this message to the editor or agent: "I don't trust you."

How do you deal with writer's block?

—Hannah

My dream is to become a successful author, but when I start to write, I always get hit by bad writers block. Any suggestions?

—Kai

Jill: Writer's block happens to pretty much everyone at some point. If I'm in the beginning of a new story, I like to take some time to plot the book out. Come up with my act one, two, and three, and how the story will end. If I know those things, sometimes it's enough to keep me going. Sometimes it's not, though. I'm stuck right now in my book. I need a little, one-page scene to finish a chapter and I just don't want to write it. I have three choices.

1. Do nothing. Ignore the problem and get nothing done. (This will only work for so long if you're on a deadline.)

2. Skip the scene and keep writing the story. I can always come back and write the tough scene later.

3. Make myself write the tough scene.

Keep in mind, it could be that you're stuck because there's something boring about the scene that needs written. If that's the case, brainstorm a twist that will make the scene more exciting.

Stephanie: I don't want to curse myself by writing this, but I haven't suffered much from writer's block. And maybe that's the "seat of the pants" writer in me—if I've written myself into a corner somehow, that's typically when I come up with my creative plot twists because I have to figure out how to get myself out.

I certainly have days when writing feels harder, or when I'm being lazy. Usually I set my timer for twenty-five minutes and tell myself that for the next twenty-five minutes I'm not going to check email or blog or browse the internet, I'm just going to write. Those first couple hundred words I write might be tough, but after that I get into the story and I'm ready to keep going.

Was there a novel you wrote that felt like *the one*, or was it something someone said that convinced you you were ready to go for it?

—**Rachelle**

Stephanie: Sadly, I learned by trial and error whether I was ready or not ready for publication. Any time I finished a project, I sent out queries. When the rejections came, one or two of the industry professionals were kind enough to give feedback of some sort. And usually—especially early on when my errors would have been glaring to anyone with experience—it resonated with me and I knew I wasn't yet ready, that I had things to fix. I could tell I was improving and getting closer, but it was still a huge shock to me when an agent called and offered representation. It was like, "Oh, I'm ready now? It's good enough?"

Me, Just Different was the first project that I felt like, "This is it—this is something bigger." I was right in the end, but I still spent four years laboring over it, and it went through a couple massive rewrites, so it still wasn't an easy road.

I always worry that my ideas might be following the ideas from other books too much.

—**Liam**

Jill: It's always tough to come up with an original idea. With as many books as there are in print, there are pretty much no new ideas. But every year there are new bestsellers. Someone always comes up with something clever. If you catch yourself following a plot of a book you've read, ask yourself what you can do to make your idea new and fresh. Brainstorm a different spin on the old idea.

For example, a while back I was sitting around feeling jealous about Suzanne Collins and her *Hunger Games* idea. I just kept thinking how brilliant it was and how she really came up with a new and fresh idea. But the more I thought about it, the more I came to see that the plot had been done before. It's a gladiator fight to the death and a love triangle. But it's the way she put those old plots together that makes it work so well.

So don't worry if your idea has been done before. Find a way to make it different and unique.

Should I finish the whole series first before I submit the first book to a publisher?
—Robert

Jill: It's up to you. I don't. Because the thing is, with most writers, their first novel isn't the one to get published. Mine wasn't. And if I'd taken the time to write the whole series of six books (which is now only four), I wouldn't have written the other books I wrote, two of which are now published.

So I like to write the first book, then write a one-paragraph overview of the other books in the series, then start submitting. Most publishers will only buy the first book, anyway. If it sells well, they'll buy the rest of the series. If it doesn't sell well, they don't have to lose money on a series.

Are there any common problems teenage authors experience that I could be watching out for? I really don't want to ruin a great story with terrible writing, because I love my story. I just want to be equipped to tell it.
—Jake

Jill: It's great that you respect the craft of writing enough to ask such a question. The most common problems I see with new writers (be they sixteen or sixty) are: being in a hurry to be published and thinking they've written the most amazing book on the planet.

Here's the thing. Thousands of books are published every year. Some are horrible. Most of them fall somewhere between just okay and good. Few become bestsellers. Don't be in a hurry. Many new writers rush things because they just want to hold a novel with their name on it. But in rushing things you skip over the learning process and make more mistakes that way. And you often end up with a book that you later wish never existed. So take the time to learn the craft of writing. Respect your chosen career and train for it. Finish your novel, edit it, join a critique group and get feedback on your book, rewrite it again, and attend a writers conference.

Mentioning writers conferences brings me to the second danger zone for new writers. I attended my first conference in 2004 and thought my book was going to be the next bestseller. Until an agent rejected me without even looking at my writing. (Gasp!) But when I stepped back to reality and took an honest look at the situation, I knew that I'd spent more time daydreaming how successful I was going to be than I'd spent working on my book.

Writing is a job. It's fun. But it's also hard work.

Doctors go to school for years before anyone lets them operate. Why did I think I could write a book without any specialized education and be a success? I'll tell you why. Because of success stories of authors like Christopher Paolini and Stephenie Meyer. But I came to realize that those situations are the one-in-a-million. For most authors, hard work brings success. So I became determined to work hard. And my hard work has paid off.

And if you want to succeed as an author, you need to become determined too. Work hard. Learn. And have fun. If you do this, you'll greatly increase your chances of publication.

Acknowledgements

From Stephanie

A big thank you to all the writers who hang out at Go Teen Writers and make it such a great community to be a part of. This book wouldn't exist without your great questions and your clear dedication to pursuing a literary life.

Jill Williamson, your heart and creativity and hard work add so much to the Go Teen Writers team. I'm so grateful for the excuse to talk to you so much.

Roseanna White, thank you for encouraging the Go Teen Writers idea many moons ago and for commenting on those early posts so I didn't feel so lonely. Also, thank you for taking time out of your very busy life to edit and fine-tune this book.

Chris Kolmorgen, thanks for your sharp editing eye, encouraging comments, and all the great insights you provided. And for the grace when I thought Harry Potter was omniscient.

Thank you Gillian Adams, Rachelle Rea, and Ellyn Gibbs for your sharp eyes and willingness to work on a tight schedule.

And thank you to Sandra Bishop, my agent, for encouraging this book, for always being in my corner, and for making time for impromptu pool side conversations that I desperately needed, even if I kept saying, "I'm fine! I'm doing great!"

Many thanks also go to my husband, Ben, who vacuums, folds laundry, and lovingly encourages me even on my most dramatic, weepy, why-am-I-doing-this? writer girl days. And to McKenna and Connor who put up with having a writer for a mom, and who remind me the real world can be pretty fun too.

Also to my fantastic grandparents team. Thank you Mom, Dad, Ann, and Bruce for coming to the house weekly so I can write.

From Jill

Thanks to Stephanie Morrill, who let me come and share in the great community she created at Go Teen Writers. I'm so glad that one guy *nudge, nudge* wanted us to meet. You're a fabulous writer and a fabulous friend.

Thanks to every teen writer out there. I love that you dream and create stories. Don't ever stop, even when you're not a teen anymore. And thanks especially to those of you who've found us online or at writers conferences. I love hearing about your stories. Keep on writing!

Thanks to Roseanna and Chris for editing our book and to Ellyn, Gillian, and Rachelle for your sharp proofreading eyes. We couldn't have published this book without you. You are all quite brilliant.

Thanks to Amanda Luedeke, my agent, who listens to all my random ideas and who graciously supported this project. You keep me sane. I'll get a bestseller for you one of these days, Amanda. I promise. ☺

Thanks to my family, who knows more than they ever wanted to about books and the publishing industry. Brad, who does laundry, cooks, and listens to my ramblings; Luke, who helps me brainstorm and builds Lego robots for my inspiration; and Kailtyn, who makes me smile and is always quick to find me a box of tissues when I'm not smiling. I love you all.

Come hang out with us!

Contests, encouragement, and community
for young writers.

www.GoTeenWriters.com
And join the community of writers on Facebook:
http://www.facebook.com/groups/goteenwriters

Skylar thought her life was perfect...

Skylar Hoyt is a girl who seems to have it all – she's pretty, popular, and has a great-looking boyfriend. Her senior year should be the best one yet. But a horrible experience at a summer party has changed everything. Now she's vowing to make better choices, including going back to church. But as Skylar tries to gain new perspective on life, the world as she knows it begins to fall apart.

Her parents are constantly fighting. Her younger sister has a big secret that Skylar is forced to keep. The guy she's dating is obsessively jealous. And the new guy down the street is ... well, not as annoying as she wants to believe he is.

In the midst of the chaos, Skylar starts to wonder who her real friends are and, even more importantly, who **she** is.

Read sample chapters and learn more about
The Reinvention of Skylar Hoyt series at:

www.StephanieMorrill.com

THE SAFE LANDS

CAPTIVES

JILL WILLIAMSON

A young man must find a cure
for a deadly disease by befriending
a beautiful woman who is his enemy.